THE MODERN WORLD

Edited by Tim Cooke

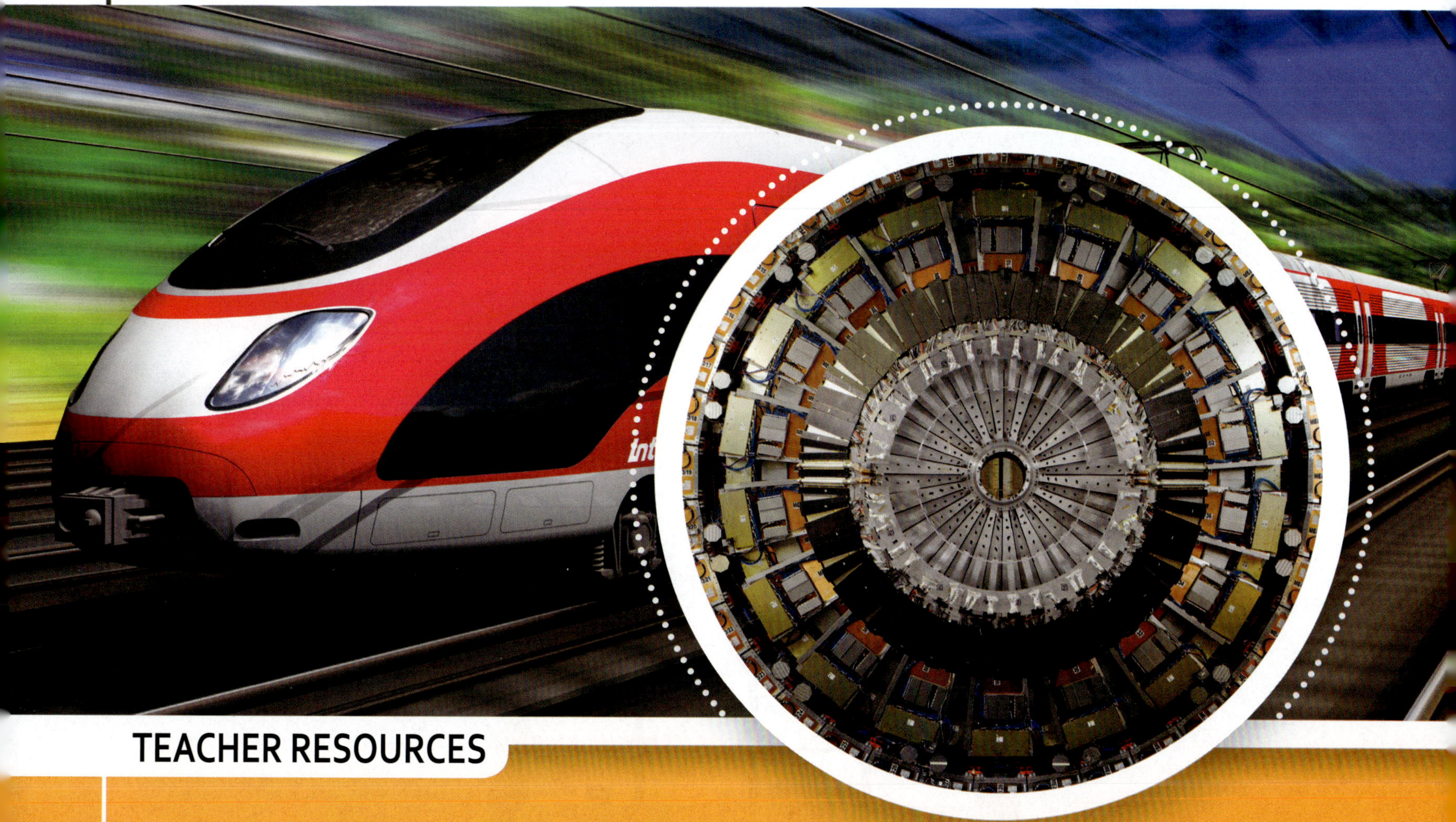

TEACHER RESOURCES

SCIENTIFIC DISCOVERY

LIGHTBOX
openlightbox.com

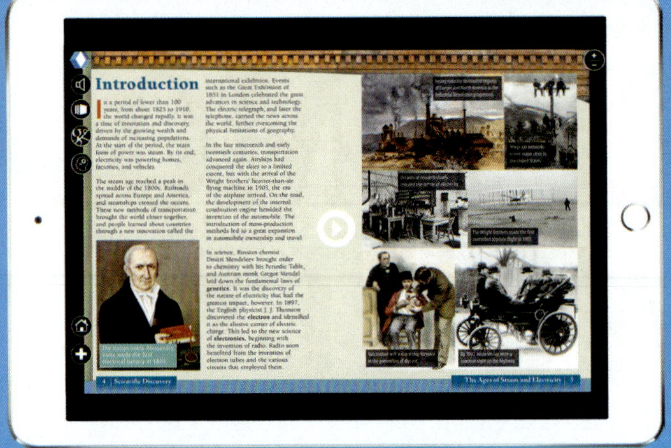

Lightbox is an all-inclusive digital solution for the teaching and learning of curriculum topics in an original, groundbreaking way. Lightbox is based on National Curriculum Standards.

STANDARD FEATURES OF LIGHTBOX

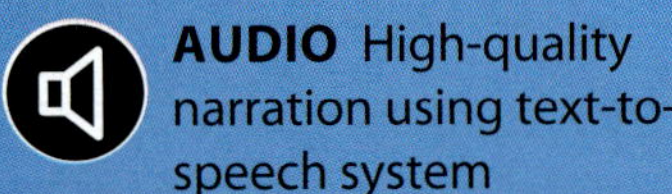

AUDIO High-quality narration using text-to-speech system

VIDEOS Embedded high-definition video clips

ACTIVITIES Printable PDFs that can be emailed and graded

WEBLINKS Curated links to external, child-safe resources

SLIDESHOWS Pictorial overviews of key concepts

TRANSPARENCIES Step-by-step layering of maps, diagrams, charts, and timelines

INTERACTIVE MAPS Interactive maps and aerial satellite imagery

QUIZZES Ten multiple choice questions that are automatically graded and emailed for teacher assessment

KEY WORDS Matching key concepts to their definitions

MORE Extra information and details on the subject

FIRST HAND Letters, diaries, and other primary sources

DOCS Speeches, newspaper articles, and other historical documents

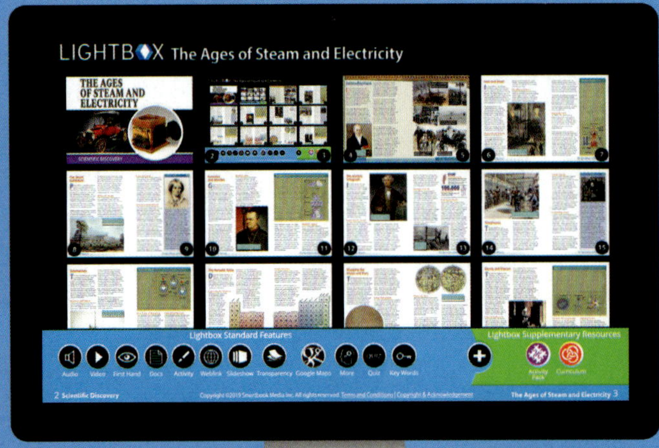

Contents

Introduction

By 1960, the globe was divided by the Cold War. This was a prolonged period of tension that had begun after the end of World War II (1939–1945). The ideological struggle pitted Western nations led by the United States against communist countries led by the Soviet Union. The Cold War saw a series of smaller conflicts, such as the Vietnam War (1955–1975), involving allies of the two superpowers. However, it inspired the development of new weapons systems, such as guided missiles and refined nuclear warheads. Exploration of space advanced rapidly, initially as a competition between Cold War combatants, but later in collaboration. Rockets were used to venture into the upper atmosphere, space probes were sent to investigate other planets, and the Apollo program landed American astronauts on the **Moon** in 1969. Astronomy advanced with the Hubble Space Telescope (HST) and other instruments in Earth orbit. Space stations such as the International Space Station (ISS) allowed scientists to live for extended periods in orbit.

From the 1960s, space probes began visiting celestial bodies such as Jupiter's moon, Europa.

For millions of people, technological advances in personal computers, cell phones, the World Wide Web, and satellite communications brought about a revolution in their daily lives in the 1980s and 1990s. In physics, researchers sought superconductors that would function at ever higher temperatures. Scientists also refined solid-state devices to make computers, tablets, and smartphones smaller, yet ever more powerful.

Medical care was also improved by the introduction of advanced techniques, such as ultrasound and organ transplants. In 2001, the **Human Genome Project** mapped the complete human genetic map. There was also a growing awareness of the effect that human activity is having on Earth, such as the threat of **global warming**. The search for more efficient renewable energy resources was at the forefront of research. The twenty-first century brought considerable challenges for the survival of humanity, for which the scientists of the future must find answers.

During the Cold War, both the United States and the Soviet Union tested powerful nuclear bombs.

Cold War attempts to dominate space led to a series of huge advances in technology.

The first personal computers appeared in offices and homes during the 1980s.

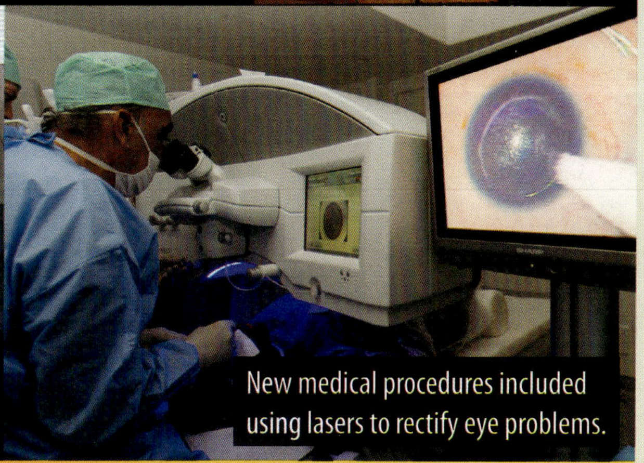

New medical procedures included using lasers to rectify eye problems.

International efforts to reduce global warming targeted industrial pollution but proved controversial.

Genetics led to a better understanding of hereditary conditions and their possible treatment or prevention.

ACTIVITIES

Video

STS Overview

Review this 1977 video discussing the development and testing of the space shuttle.

1. Which organizations were most heavily involved in the creation of the space shuttle? Why would they be involved in its development?
2. What design goals did the developers of the space shuttles likely have in mind? Did the space shuttle successfully meet these goals? In what ways did the system succeed or fail?

Weblink

Science in the Modern World

Explore the development of some of the main themes in science and technology since the 1960s.

1. Why are these developments or inventions noteworthy? What effect would they have on human advancements in this field?
2. What factors would lead to the creation of these technologies? Are these factors similar for each development? If not, how would they differ?
3. Would any of these developments influence the creation of any others? How?

RUBRIC

Sketch a Design Solution

As a group, identify a simple design solution to the difficulties of enabling someone to act as an eyewitness observer at a nuclear test, where explosive force and radioactive fallout are going to be a problem. Brainstorm possible solutions and select the best design solution. Make a sketch of a model or prototype. An exemplary project will meet the following criteria:

- The problem is defined in detail
- All constraints are listed
- Possible solutions from the brainstorming session are listed
- Two or three ideas are selected from brainstormed list
- Sketches are created for the selected idea
- Sketches are labeled with dimensions and materials for each component
- Detailed list of materials is included
- Detailed procedures are included
- Hypothesis following an "if.., then..." format is developed for the design
- Strengths of the design are listed
- Weaknesses of the design or compromises of the design are listed
- The chosen design effectively addresses the identified problem
- Modifications to the design are documented
- Presentation is well-organized
- Presentation is clearly communicated visually with appropriate data, sketches, graphs or pictures
- Presentation includes contributions from all team members

The first hydrogen bomb blasted a crater 6,230 feet (1.7 kilometers) across and 164 feet (50 meters) deep.

Nuclear Weapons

In August 1945, a new and devastating bomb was dropped on the Japanese cities of Hiroshima and Nagasaki. This was the atomic bomb, the first nuclear weapon. A few years later, an even more destructive nuclear weapon, the hydrogen bomb, was developed.

The basis for the development of nuclear weapons was laid by British physicist Ernest Rutherford, who discovered that the atoms of some elements could be "split" to form other elements. Then, in 1939, the German chemists, Otto Hahn and Fritz Strassmann, split the uranium atom. The process released a vast amount of energy, as predicted by German physicist Albert Einstein. If a reaction of this type could be performed on a larger scale, a chain reaction would produce an immensely powerful explosion.

Research into nuclear weapons was not a priority in Germany at the time. In World War II, however, the United States set up the Manhattan Project. Led by J. Robert Oppenheimer, nuclear physicists produced an atomic bomb in July 1945. Initially, only the United States had the atomic bomb.

In 1949, the Soviet Union tested its own atomic bomb. Great Britain, France, and China also quickly developed weapons of this type. By 2015, North Korea, India, Pakistan, and Israel possessed nuclear weapons in addition to the original powers.

The Hydrogen Bomb

In 1941, two U.S. physicists, Enrico Fermi and Edward Teller, realized that it would be possible to use the energy from an atomic bomb to trigger an even more powerful nuclear reaction. This weapon would fuse together atoms of deuterium, a rare form of hydrogen. In 1949, when the Soviet Union developed an atomic bomb, the United States decided to build this new hydrogen bomb. Edward Teller and Stanislaw Ulam designed the device, which was successfully tested on November 1, 1952. A single hydrogen bomb could produce an explosion equivalent to millions of tons of conventional explosives. By August 1953, the Russians also had a hydrogen bomb.

Tactical Nuclear Weapons

The first nuclear weapons were too large and heavy to transport easily on the battlefield. In the 1950s, however, the United States and the Soviet Union (USSR) developed nuclear weapons small enough to be fired from artillery pieces or carried by fighter aircraft. These weapons, which are designed to be used against military forces rather than large civilian targets, are called tactical nuclear weapons.

The Hydrogen Bomb

In late 1952, U.S. scientists tested the first hydrogen bomb in an operation codenamed Ivy Mike. The test took place at Eniwetok Atoll in the Marshall Islands in the Pacific Ocean. The bomb itself, nicknamed Mike, used deuterium as its fuel. It detonated with more than 500 times the force of the atomic bombs dropped on Hiroshima and Nagasaki at the end of World War II. This hydrogen bomb, sometimes called a thermonuclear bomb, worked by **fusion**, or crashing atoms together. Previous atomic bombs had worked by fission, or splitting atoms. The new weapon destroyed the tiny island where it was detonated and also released huge amounts of radioactive fallout into the atmosphere. Military personnel wearing protective goggles witnessed the test. They later claimed the radioactivity had damaged their health.

ACTIVITIES

Video

Ivy Mike Hydrogen Bomb Detonation

Review the video of the Ivy Mike detonation.

1. What effect would seeing such a powerful explosion closeup have had on witnesses? Might their view of military weapons research have been altered in any way? What might have been the reaction today?
2. After the testing of the first atomic bomb in 1945, Robert Oppenheimer quoted from the Bhagavad-Gita "I am become death, the shatterer of worlds." What could be concluded from such a statement?

Weblink

The Development and Proliferation of Nuclear Weapons

Analyze the article about the development and proliferation of nuclear weapons.

1. Why did Albert Einstein write to President Franklin D. Roosevelt just after the outbreak of World War II? How might his situation as an escapee from Nazi Germany have had a bearing on the letter?
2. Why did President Harry S. Truman decide to drop such a destructive nuclear weapon on a Japanese city?
3. What reasons might there be for making the bombing of civilian populations part of modern warfare? Is behavior like this ever justified? Defend a position.
4. How effective are non-proliferation agreements (NPTs)? Is it possible for all countries of the world to agree to such an agreement? Assess the effectiveness of such agreements to date.

RUBRIC

Writing a Telegram

Students will research the development of intercontinental ballistic missiles in the United States and the Soviet Union and write a telegram from the point of view of someone experiencing a test launch. An exemplary telegram will meet the following criteria:

- Chooses an appropriate and relevant recipient for the telegram
- Focuses on a specific, well-defined topic
- Begins with a strong opening to engage the reader
- Introduces varied details to express the feelings of the writer
- Provides an insightful view into the chosen time period
- Writes with a unique, engaging voice and perspective
- Expresses thoughts and information using complete and varied sentence structure
- Utilizes appropriate phrasing and terminology for the time period
- Uses descriptive words and phrases to create vivid imagery and keep the reader engaged
- Includes a proper salutation and closing statement
- Uses correct spelling, grammar, and punctuation

Guided Missiles

During World War II, the Germans made significant advances in the development of guided missiles. After the war, both the United States and the Soviet Union used German technology and German scientists to build their own guided missiles. Advances in electronics, sensors, and computers made guided missiles a dominant weapon on the modern battlefield.

In the United States, attention focused on developing a surface-to-air missile (SAM) capable of destroying enemy aircraft. By 1953, the United States. had developed the Nike Ajax air defense missile. The missile was large, and could only be fired from fixed installations. A motor accelerated the missile to speeds faster than sound, when a smaller rocket took over. This design was widely used in later SAMs. **Radar** beams tracked both the missile and the target, sending information to a computer that guided the missile. In 1954, the Soviet Union deployed its own SAM, the SA-1, which was guided by radar inside the missile itself. Both the United States and the Soviet Union went on to develop SAMs that were smaller and effective at greater distances.

Intercontinental Missiles

Until the 1950s, the United States and the Soviet Union both based their defenses on heavy bombers. The bombers would attack the enemy homelands in the event of a war. The development of SAMs reduced the chances of bombers penetrating enemy missile defense systems.

During the Cold War, Soviet missiles were displayed during huge military parades through Moscow.

The V-1 Flying Bomb

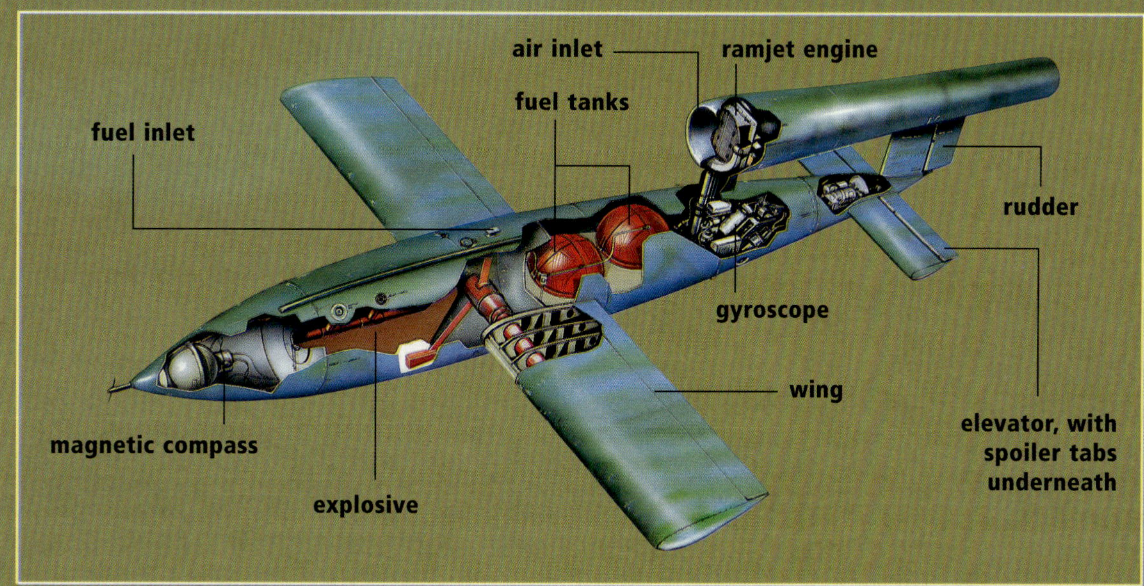

German scientists built the V-1 in World War II to attack enemy targets. It was the first "cruise missile," with a speed of 350 miles per hour (560 kilometers per hour) and a range of 160 miles (260 km). The V-1 had a small jet engine, and was steered using elevators and a rudder at the rear. It was guided by a compass linked to a **gyroscope**. After flying a preset distance, the V-1 was put into a dive by the spoiler tabs on the tail section. The engine then cut out. The United States experimented with cruise missiles in the 1950s, but it was only in the 1970s that computers and electronics allowed the creation of accurate systems of navigation that could be incorporated in modern cruise missiles.

In response, both countries developed intercontinental ballistic missiles (ICBMs) armed with nuclear warheads. These are multistage rockets similar to those used to put satellites into orbit. Rocket engines power the missile to the edge of space. The warhead follows an arc before striking its target.

Throughout the 1950s and 1960s, the United States and Soviet Union developed ICBMs with greater ranges and more powerful warheads.

The Soviet SS-9 was the first ICBM to carry multiple warheads. This technology was adopted in the U.S. Minuteman III missile of 1970. The missile carried multiple warheads anchored to a structure called a "bus" that could direct each warhead to a different target. Nearly all modern ICBMs carry these Multiple Independently Targetable Reentry Vehicles (MIRVs). MIRVs allow a single missile to destroy many targets over a wide area.

ACTIVITIES

Weblink

Intercontinental Ballistic Missiles

Analyze the article about the development of ICBMs:

1. Why are ICBMs so effective? Is there any way for countries to defend against an attack by ICBMs? Should such weapons ever be used either offensively or as deterrents? Explain your reasons for or against.
2. Why did German engineers help the United States to develop ballistic missile weapons after World War II? Consider what their motives might have been.
3. Compare ICBMs and Cruise missiles. What are the advantages and disadvantages of one type of missile over the other. Justify your conclusions.

Planetary Probes

In the late 1950s, the Soviet Union and then the United States launched satellites into orbit and sent probes to the Moon. These first spacecraft did not visit other planets, but they sent back important data from space. They also helped develop the technology for a series of far more ambitious missions.

Venus

First visited: December 1962

Distance from Earth: 162 million miles (261 million km)

Key missions:
1962 Mariner 2 (U.S.) flyby
1970 Venera 7 (USSR) first landing
1975 Venera 9 (USSR) into orbit
1985 Vega 1, Vega 2 (USSR) dropped instruments to surface
1990 Magellan (U.S.) mapped surface
2006 Venus Express (U.S.) studied atmosphere and mapped surface

Mars

First visited: July 1965

Distance from Earth: 33.9 million miles (54.6 million km)

Key missions:
1965 Mariner 4 (U.S.) flyby
1971 Mariner 9 (U.S.) into orbit
1976 Viking 1, Viking 2 (U.S.) orbiters with landers
2004 Spirit and Opportunity (U.S.) Mars rovers explored surface

Uncrewed probes visited the Moon in 1959. The next targets were Earth's closest neighbors, Venus and Mars, in the 1960s and 1970s. They were followed by the gas giants, Jupiter and Saturn. Finally, probes reached the outer planets, Uranus and Neptune, and the dwarf planet Pluto.

Gas Giants

First visited: 1973 (Jupiter), 1979 (Saturn)

Distance from Earth: 365 million miles (588 million km) Jupiter, 746 million miles (1.2 billion km) Saturn

Key missions:

1973 Pioneer 10 (U.S.) flyby Jupiter
1979 Pioneer 11 (U.S.) flyby Saturn
1995 Galileo (U.S.) orbiter and probe on Jupiter
2004 Cassini–Huygens (U.S.) orbiter and probe on Saturn and its moon, Titan

Outer Planets

First visited: 1986 (Uranus), 1989 (Neptune), 2015 (Pluto)

Distance from Earth: 1.6 billion miles (2.6 billion km) Uranus, 2.7 billion miles (4.3 billion km) Neptune, 4.67 billion miles (7.5 billion km) Pluto

Key missions:

1986 Voyager 2 (U.S.) flyby of Uranus
1989 Voyager 2 (U.S.) flyby of Neptune
2015 New Horizons (U.S.) flyby of Pluto

More

Planetary Probes

Research online and study the uncrewed probes that visited Venus, Mars, the Gas Giants, and the Outer Planets.

1. What is the historical significance of each of these probes? Why were the United States and the Soviet Union eager to find out about these planets? Assess their reasons.
2. Is it important for scientists to collect data from other planets? Could such knowledge help to further human understanding of the universe? In what ways might it be useful in the future? Support your judgments.

RUBRIC

Analyzing a Scientific Blog

Students will complete a thorough analysis of a blog that explores scientific events. An exemplary analysis will meet the following criteria.

- Chooses a relevant and meaningful blog
- Provides a working link to the blog
- Identifies the blogger
- Presents information about the blogger
- Assesses the blogger's reliability
- Considers and assesses the blogger's perspective
- Determines the blogger's intended audience
- Determines whether the blogger had firsthand knowledge of the topic or event, or whether he or she is reporting as a secondary source
- Summarizes the events that the blogger is covering
- Determines any bias present in the blog postings
- Examines and evaluates any content tags used by the blogger
- Uses additional sources to confirms any claims made by the blog
- Uses correct spelling, grammar, and punctuation

Semiconductors

Most metals conduct electricity well. Electrical wires are often made from copper, for example. Other substances, including glass, paper, and rubber, conduct electricity very badly and so are used to insulate electrical wiring. Between the extremes of conductors and insulators are substances called semiconductors. They include tin, germanium, selenium, and zinc. The most widely used semiconductor material is silicon. Semiconductors are used to make components for electronic devices, such as radios, TVs, and computers.

A semiconductor is sometimes an insulator, but under some conditions it allows an electric current to flow through it. Scientists studying electricity in the 1830s found that some substances lost conductivity if they were heated. Some poor conductors, meanwhile, would allow a current to flow in one direction only when light was shone onto them.

The Rectifier

When Italian physicist Guglielmo Marconi explored ways to convert an electrical current into radio waves in the early 1900s, he used a device called a rectifier to detect incoming radio signals. The rectifier allows a current to flow in only one direction. It had been invented by German physicist Ferdinand Braun in 1874, using a crystal of **galena**. This was the crystal in the first radio receivers, known as "crystal sets." Braun's rectifier was also the first semiconductor device.

Valves and Transistors

Rectifiers have two terminals, but radio technology required devices with three terminals. These allowed the current or voltage between two of the terminals to be controlled by the current or voltage applied to the third. The first three-terminal devices were vacuum tube triodes, called valves. Later versions had several triodes enclosed in the same tube.

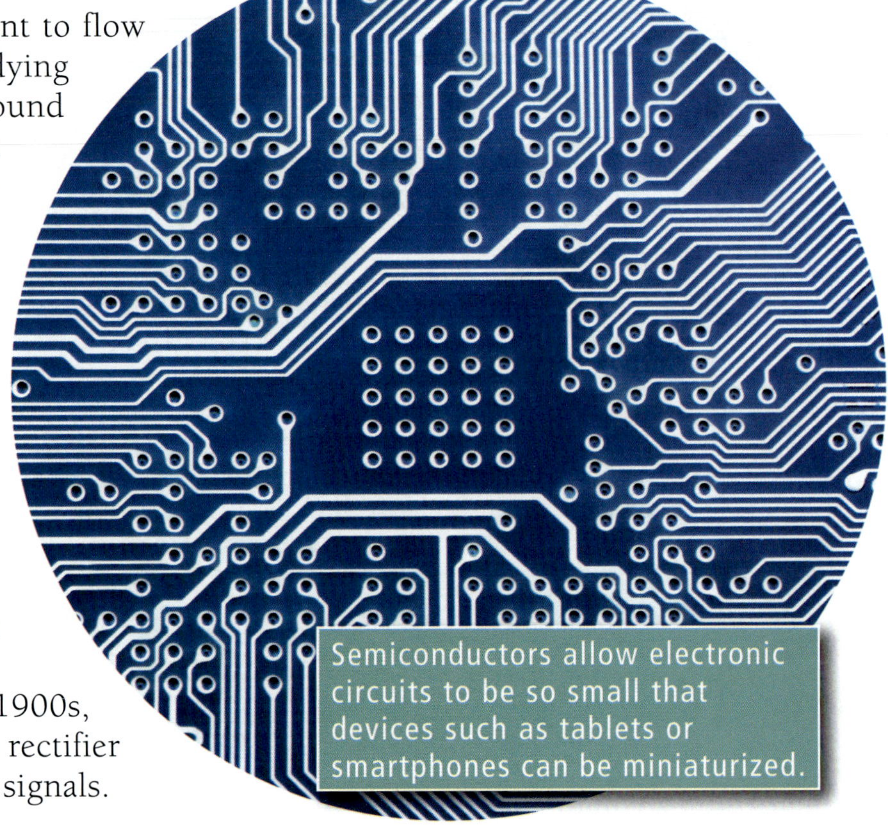

Semiconductors allow electronic circuits to be so small that devices such as tablets or smartphones can be miniaturized.

In 1947, three physicists, English-born American William Shockley and Americans John Bardeen and Walter Brattain, made the first solid three-terminal **transistor** using germanium. In 1948, they used their transistors to make an audio **amplifier**. That same year, Shockley conceived the junction transistor, made from slices of semiconductor material pressed together. He found that impurities in the germanium crystal improved its semiconductor properties.

Types of Semiconductors

Modern semiconductors are made from slices of silicon crystal with low concentrations of impurities added. If arsenic is added, each arsenic atom links to four silicon atoms, leaving one surplus electron. Electrons carry a negative charge, so this is known as an n-type semiconductor. If boron is added to silicon, all the available electrons are used, leaving a vacancy or "hole" for a positively charged proton. This is known as a p-type semiconductor. Applying a current makes the free electrons move in one direction through an n-type semiconductor, and causes the holes to move in the opposite direction through a p-type semiconductor.

There are silicon chips in all modern electronic devices. The chips are minute plastic cases enclosing layers of transistors and related components, together with the wiring linking them, on the surface of a sliver of silicon. They are integrated circuits based on semiconductor technology.

Jack Kilby

Jack Kilby was an American electronic engineer who worked at Texas Instruments. In 1958, he realized that, rather than making transistors one at a time, he could overlay different impurities in order to make several transistors together and place them on the same semiconductor. Other electronic components, such as **diodes**, capacitors, and resistors, could then be added to complete a whole circuit. Kilby had invented the integrated circuit. Kilby's invention rapidly led to further advances. Just a year later, at Fairchild Semiconductor Corporation, Swiss physicist Jean Hoerni and American electronic engineer Robert Noyce developed planar technology. This process spreads different layers of semiconductors and impurities onto a wafer of silicon to make a flat transistor, then evaporates metal strips onto the surface to make the necessary connections for the device to function.

ACTIVITIES

First Hand

A Look at the Semiconductor Industry

Review this blog on the semi-conductor industry.

1. Why is the semiconductor industry such a major part of the economy? Assess what the next technological advance in semiconductors might be.
2. What are transistors? Why might selenium have been important in the development of semiconductors?

Weblink

Semiconductors

Analyze this weblink description of semiconductors

1. What is a semiconductor? Explain the answer in your own words.
2. Which element is the best-known semiconductor and why? What are the major uses for semiconductors, and how might their discovery have been considered to have advanced human civilization? Describe 10 uses for semiconductors in the modern world.

RUBRIC

Analyzing a Magazine Article

Students will fine and assess a magazine article about the various different types of medical scanners and write an analysis. An exemplary analysis will meet the following criteria:

- Identifies the topic of the article
- Identifies the main points and opinions presented in the article
- Identifies the writer of the article
- Presents information about the writer and infers how his or her life may have shaped this opinion
- Assesses the writer's reliability
- Analyzes how the writer makes his or her argument
- Uses evidence from the article to show how the writer supports his or her argument
- Analyzes the writer's use of literary devices to enhance the article
- Differentiates between the facts and opinions presented in the article
- Identifies when and where the article was published, and determines its intended audience
- Identifies and understands the goals of the article
- Assesses the effectiveness of the format in presenting the writer's argument
- Connects the article to the societal and historical context in which it was written
- Infers what is not said about this topic in the article
- Identifies what information is unintentionally implied in the article

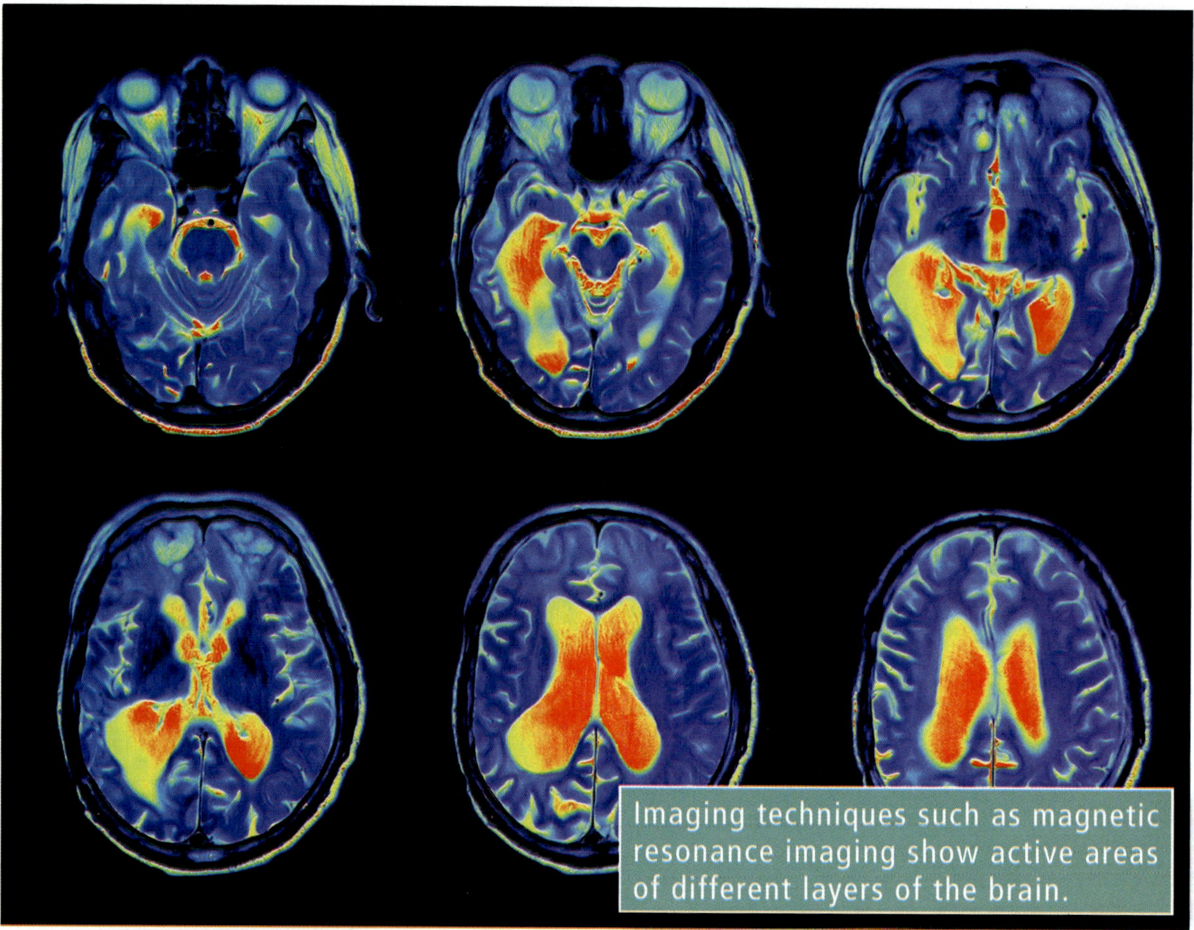

Imaging techniques such as magnetic resonance imaging show active areas of different layers of the brain.

Seeing Inside The Body

Ancient Greek doctors listened to the lungs and the heart through the chest cavity to find out what was happening inside the body. Doctors today use stethoscopes for the same purpose. Stethoscopes were invented in 1852, by U.S. physician George P. Cammann. In November 1895, the German-born Dutch physicist Wilhelm Röntgen discovered X-rays, or penetrating electromagnetic radiation. X-rays penetrated soft tissue but not bones or dense matter, so they could be used to detect bone fractures. For the first time, physicians could look inside the body without the need for surgery.

In 1903, Dutch scientist Willem Einthoven performed the first electrocardiograph (ECG). He recorded the electrical activity of the heart using a string galvanometer, which measures electrical currents. In the 1920s, German biologist Hans Berger used a string galvanometer to detect brain waves. This led to the invention of electroencephalograms (EEGs). These recordings of brain activity are used to diagnose **epilepsy** and detect brain injuries.

Seeing with Sound

Since World War II, scientists have developed scanning technologies to see inside the body. One method uses ultrasound, or very high-pitched sound waves. When directed into the human body, ultrasound "bounces" off its internal structures, showing their location, shape, and size. The first ultrasound images were produced by U.S. physician Robert Lee Wild in 1952.

Scanning Methods

In 1972, U.S. physicist Allan MacLeod Cormack and U.S. computer engineer Godfrey Newbold Hounsfield together invented computed, or computerized, tomography (CT). This can detect small tumors and blood clots. In 1977, U.S. biologist and physicist Raymond Damadian took the first picture inside the human body using magnetic resonance imaging (MRI).

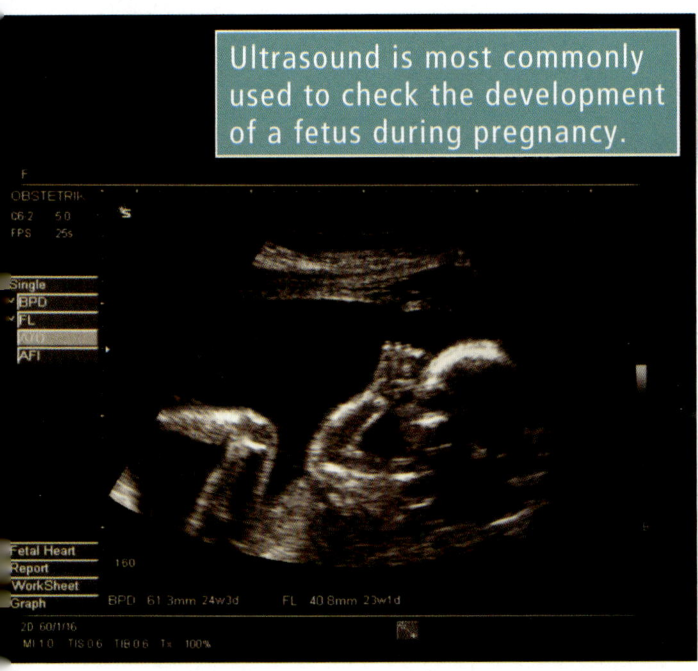

Ultrasound is most commonly used to check the development of a fetus during pregnancy.

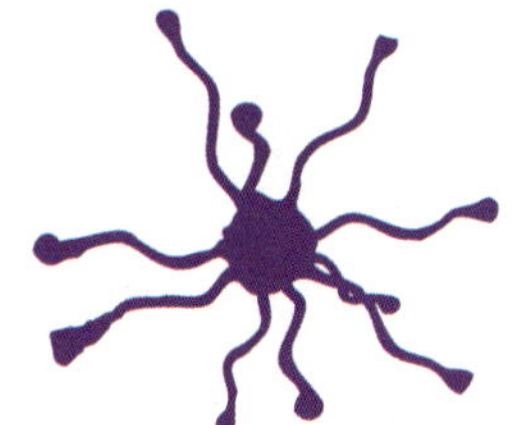

100 BILLION

The approximate number of neurons, or nerve cells, that make up the human brain

100 TIMES

The increase in detail between traditional X-rays and modern CT scans

This technique is effective in imaging damage to soft tissues such as muscles and nerves. MRI scans reveal information about the biological activity of the tissues. CT and MRI paved the way for positron emission tomography (PET) scanning.

PET tracks brain activity, so it is useful for studying mental illness and locating brain tumors. The patient is first injected with a weak radioactive substance that gives off positrons, or positively charged electrons. The radioactive substance collects in biologically active parts of the body, such as the brain. As the positrons collide with electrons in the brain tissue, they emit shortwave gamma rays. PET sensors around the patient's head detect the rays, and a computer uses the data to produce cross-sections of the brain that can be made into a three-dimensional image. PET can give information about which parts of the brain are active when a person is working, listening, reading, or sleeping.

ACTIVITIES

Weblink

Medical Imaging

Analyze this weblink about medical scanners.

1. Compare the factors driving the medical imaging market with the factors inhibiting the growth of medical imaging. Do the advantages outweigh the disadvantages? Describe the arguments for and against.
2. How do medical scanners interface with other digital medical applications? Assess the increasing importance of medical imaging in today's healthcare.

Advanced Surgery

Modern surgery is able to cure many of the illnesses and diseases that once caused suffering or even death. Advanced surgical methods include organ transplants, where organs such as hearts, kidneys, or eyes are transferred from one patient to another, and the fitting of artificial body parts.

Organ Transplants

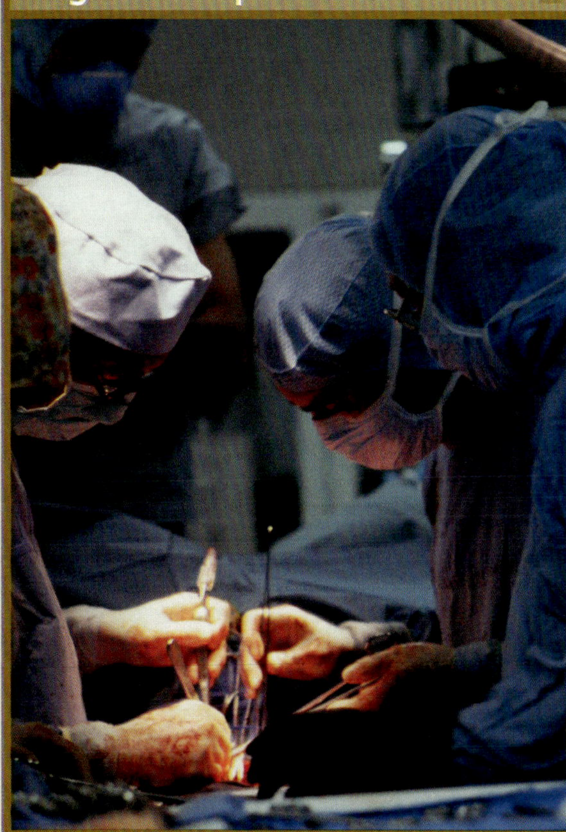

Breakthrough: First heart transplant

When carried out: 1967

Where carried out: Cape Town, South Africa

Pioneer: Christiaan Barnard

Significance: Led to the development of routine heart transplants. In 2015, more than 30,000 transplants were carried out in the United States, of which about 2,000 were heart transplants.

Artificial Body Parts

Breakthrough: First steel-and-Teflon artificial hip

When introduced: 1960

Where introduced: Great Britain

Inventor: Sir John Charnley

Significance: Replaced problematic plastic-and-acrylic joints with more reliable, freer-moving alternative. When the plastic RCH 1000 replaced Teflon, hip replacement became even more successful. Artificial hips are now the most commonly used artificial body replacements.

ACTIVITIES

Surgeons also use noninvasive techniques to examine and treat the body. When they do not have to make large cuts to perform surgery, the patient recovers more quickly. This was made possible by a device called an **endoscope** and the use of **lasers** rather than traditional scalpels to make incisions.

Noninvasive Surgery

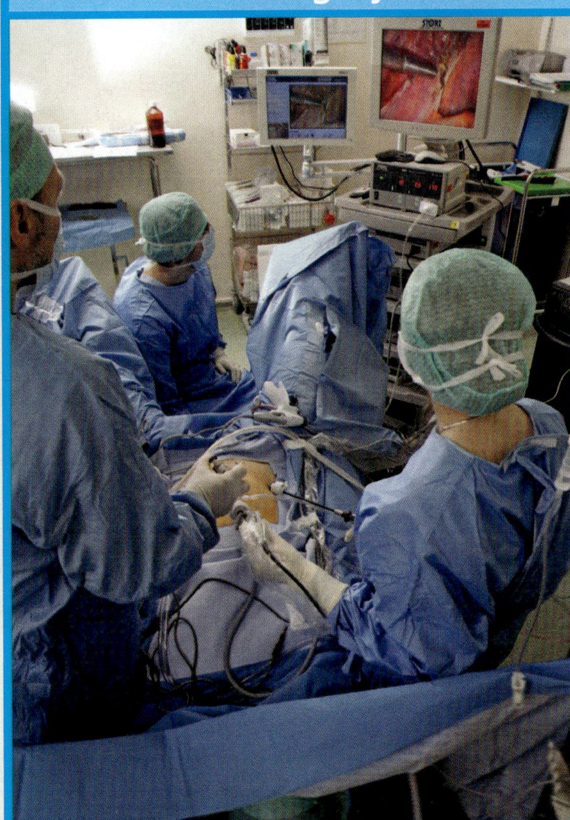

Breakthrough: First rod-lens endoscope

When introduced: 1959

Where introduced: Great Britain

Inventor: Harold Hopkins

Significance: New design replaced bulky lens with a tube made from glass rods that act as lenses. This allowed endoscope tubes to become thinner and more flexible, allowing them to access more parts of the body, while still containing imaging devices and surgical tools, such as lasers.

Pacemakers

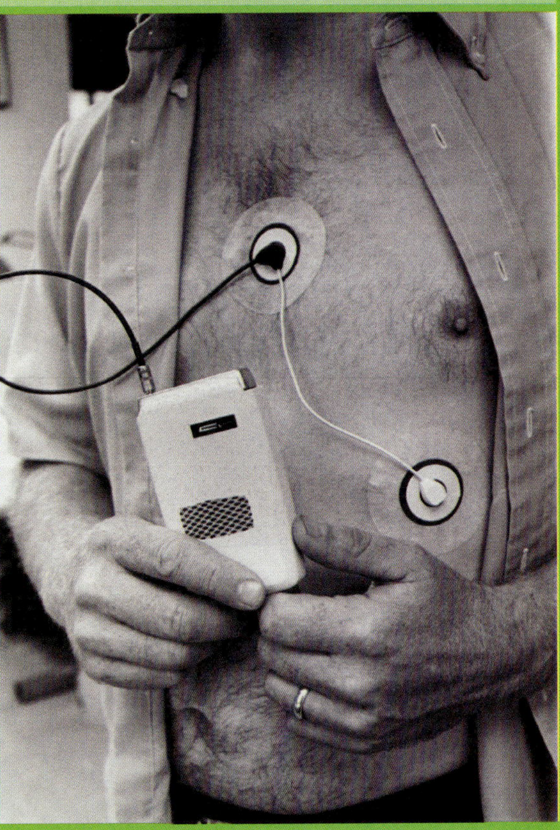

Breakthrough: First artificial pacemaker

When introduced: 1958

Where introduced: Sweden

Inventor: Ake Senning

Significance: Artificial units implanted in chest send electrical impulses to regulate the beating of the heart. The initial batteries, which lasted only two or three years, were replaced in 1988. Since then, pacemakers using nuclear power can run for 20 years before needing to be replaced.

More

Advanced Surgery

Research online and study the innovative ways in which four modern medical advancements have led to major breakthroughs in surgery: organ transplants, artificial body parts, noninvasive surgery, and pacemakers.

1. Assess which of these technologies might have had the most impact on the survival prospects and quality of life for patients? Give reasons.
2. Which of these technologies has developed most rapidly post 1960s to the present day? Summarize why this might be the case.

In a fully automated auto production line, each robot performs set tasks as a car body passes by.

Robotics

A robot is a self-controlling, automatic device that can carry out a preprogrammed task. A robot cannot learn to "think" for itself. Unlike in science-fiction movies, most real robots are not modeled on the human body.

The science of robotics dates back to about 1000 AD, when machines were built to imitate a limited range of human actions. These machines are known as automata. Today, commercial robots are used to perform jobs more cheaply, more accurately, and more reliably than humans. They are also used for tasks that are too dirty, dangerous, or dull for humans.

Programming Robots

Industrial robotics uses a combination of numerical control (NC) and teleoperator technologies. NC is a method of controlling machines with preprogrammed numbers. It was first developed during the late 1940s and early 1950s. The first NC machine tool was built in 1952 at the Massachusetts Institute of Technology.

A teleoperator is a mechanism that is controlled by a human from a remote location. Teleoperators were developed in the early 1940s to handle radioactive materials that are dangerous to humans. In some versions, the human operator moves a mechanical arm so that a duplicate robot arm moves at another location.

Production Line Robots

The first industrial robot was developed by U.S. inventor George C. Devol and businessman Joseph Engelberger. Called the Unimate, it was sold to General Motors in 1962. The robot was used to remove hot die castings from molds and for spot welding. Devol and Engelberger's company, Unimation, made more sophisticated robots capable of tasks such as spray painting.

250,000
ROBOTS
The number of industrial robots estimated to be in use in the United States in 2017

5 million
JOBS
The number of U.S. workers predicted to lose their jobs to automation in the 2020s

In the early twenty-first century, scientists began to experiment with artificial intelligence (AI) in robots. AI is computer technology that aims to enable robots to figure out how to solve problems without the need for a program. Some people find the idea of "thinking" robots troubling.

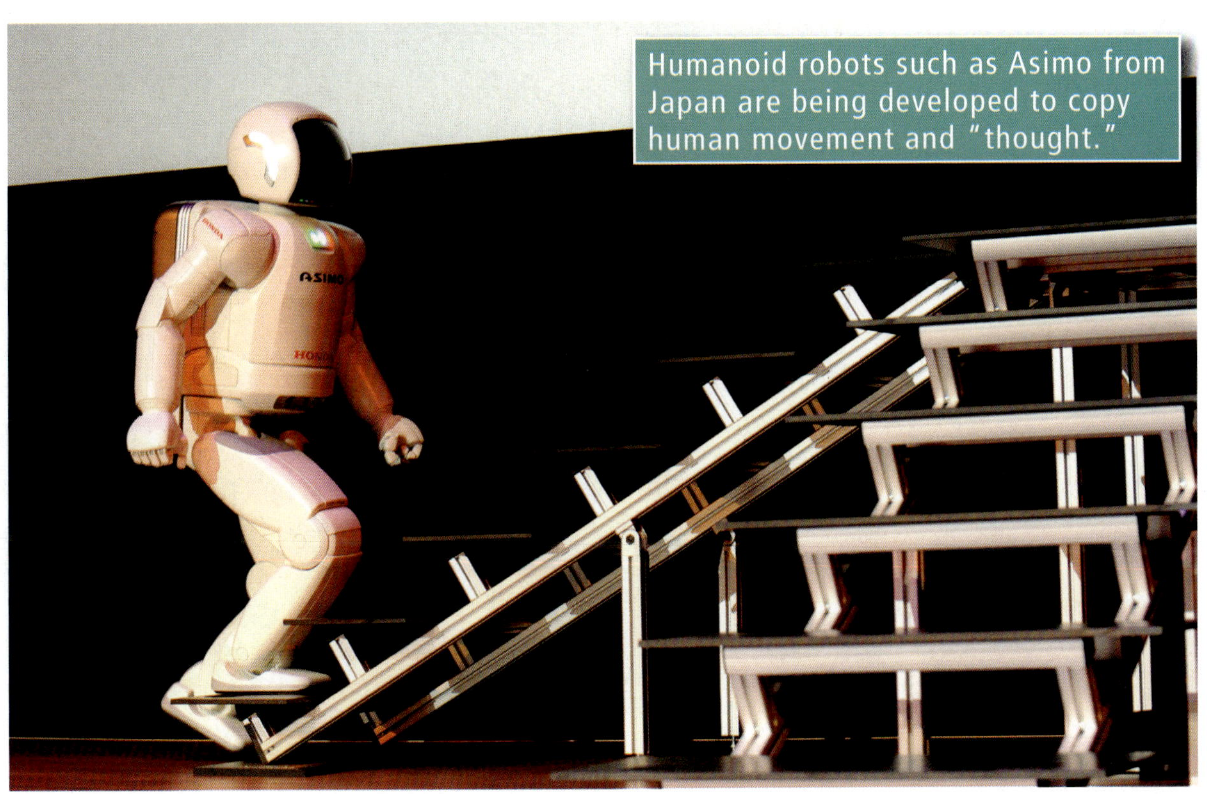

Humanoid robots such as Asimo from Japan are being developed to copy human movement and "thought."

ACTIVITIES

Video

Next Generation: Advanced Robots
Watch this video on seven of the world's most advanced human-like robots.

1. Scientists have studied all aspects of human movement to develop robots that can balance and walk on two legs. They have also developed facial expressions, "skin," and voices. Has science fiction become reality? Evaluate the technology. Assess whether or not it will have useful applications for society.
2. Discuss whether robots might eventually replace humans for most, if not all, manual tasks. What other uses might human robots have in everyday life? Will this be good or bad for society? Summarize your conclusions.

Weblink

A Brief History of Robotics Since 1950
Assess this weblink on the history of robotics since the 1950s.

1. What industrial factors might have precipitated the development of robotics in the late 1800s? Describe the types of activity the first robots were introduced to do.
2. Why did it take until the middle of the twentieth century for robots to be produced commercially? What were some of the drawbacks of the early robots? Why was "Planetbot" ultimately unsuccessful?

RUBRIC

Analyzing an Interview

Students will listen to and assess a press interview given by Neil Armstrong, Buzz Aldrin and Michael Collins upon their successful return to Earth in 1969 and write an analysis of what they have learned. An exemplary interview analysis will meet the following criteria:

- Identifies where and when the interview took place
- Identifies the subject of the interview
- Describes how the interview is presented
- Gives examples of the information provided by the interview
- Summarizes the information and opinions presented by the subject of the interview
- States whether the information is a firsthand or secondhand account
- Points out how easy or difficult to understand the subject of the interview is
- Organizes the analysis in a logical, effective manner
- Makes inferences about the experiences of the interview subjects
- Compares the interview to other sources about the same event
- Cites all sources used in the analysis
- Uses correct spelling, grammar, and punctuation

Landing on the Moon

The Moon landing was the major achievement of the Apollo program. The program began with missions to test launch procedures, rockets, and modules. It sent uncrewed and then crewed missions first into Earth orbit, and then around the Moon. In January 1967, the first planned Apollo flight ended in disaster when three astronauts died in a fire during tests on the launch pad. The following year, the National Aeronautics and Space Administration (**NASA**) completed three unmanned launches. In October 1968, *Apollo 7* carried three astronauts on a 163-orbit flight around Earth to test the command module. Two months later, *Apollo 8* took three astronauts to the Moon, where they made 10 orbits. March 1969 saw the testing of the lunar module in Earth orbit by *Apollo 9*, and in May that year, two *Apollo 10* astronauts tested the lunar module in a low orbit around the Moon.

Man on the Moon

Apollo 11 had four main parts. The giant Saturn V rocket propelled the craft into space. The command module housed the three astronauts, Neil Armstrong, Edwin "Buzz" Aldrin, and Michael Collins, on their journey to the Moon. The service module beneath the command module contained the propulsion rockets for the journey. Below the service module was the lunar module, *Eagle*.

The three-module "pack" detached from the rocket while in Earth orbit and flew to the Moon. The first stage of the rocket fell back into the ocean. In 2012, the five engines from *Apollo 11*'s Saturn V rocket were discovered on the bed of the Atlantic Ocean.

Neil Armstrong landed on the Moon saying, "That's one small step for a man, one giant leap for mankind."

Once in Moon orbit, the lunar module detached and carried Armstrong and Aldrin down to the Moon's surface. They landed in a region called the Sea of Tranquility on July 20. The men spent two hours taking photographs and collecting samples. They placed an American flag on the Moon's surface and left behind a plaque commemorating their historic visit. Once their mission was complete, they took off in *Eagle* and docked with the orbiting command module. The command module headed back to Earth and parachuted into the Pacific Ocean just eight days after it had left.

Later Apollo Missions

In November 1969, *Apollo 12* repeated the achievement of *Apollo 11*. In April 1970, however, *Apollo 13* was a near-disaster. An explosion in the service module cut off power and oxygen. The crew returned in the lunar module, moving to the command module just before making a safe reentry into Earth's atmosphere. Later missions used additional equipment on the lunar surface, carried out detailed surveys, and collected samples to take back to Earth. In July 1971, *Apollo 15* carried a Lunar Rover Vehicle to the Moon. *Apollo 17* was NASA's last crewed trip to the Moon, in December 1972.

In all, the Apollo program had cost about $25 billion. That makes the 842 pounds (382 kg) of Moon rock brought back to Earth between July 1969 and December 1972 worth more than $1.8 million per ounce (28 g).

The Moon Landing

In July 1969, it took *Apollo 11* about three days to fly from Earth to enter orbit around the Moon. On the fourth day, Neil Armstrong and Buzz Aldrin entered the lunar module, *Eagle*, to descend to the Moon. Michael Collins remained in orbit in the command module, *Columbia*. *Eagle* descended toward the landing site, which had been selected by studying photographs taken by orbiting probes. As the module neared the surface, Armstrong saw a field of boulders and had to take manual control to steer toward a smoother area. The module's computers overloaded, and alarms sounded. When the lander finally touched down, it had only 30 seconds of fuel left. Armstrong radioed back to his relieved colleagues at NASA, "The *Eagle* has landed." At 10:56 PM Eastern Daylight Time on July 20, 1969, Armstrong became the first person to step on another world. Around half a million people watched live on television around the globe.

ACTIVITIES

Video

Apollo 11 Moon Landing NASA Original Footage

Watch this documentary about the Apollo 11 Moon landing.

1. Why do you think the mission was such a spectacular moment for humankind? Do you think seeing the images of the astronauts walking on the Moon for the first time would have the same impact on viewers today? Compare how the event was covered by the media in 1969, and contrast it with how such an event might be covered today.
2. Describe the physical and psychological effects such a historic event might have had on the astronauts.

Weblink

What Was the Apollo Program?

Read this account of the Apollo program.

1. Why did the United States embark on the Apollo program? What challenge to the nation did John F. Kennedy give in 1961? Might this challenge have been prompted by political considerations? If so, assess what they might have been.
2. How many Apollo missions involved crewed space flights? After Apollo 11, how many other missions landed on the Moon? Why do you think the astronauts of those missions are not as well known as Armstrong, Aldrin, and Collins?

RUBRIC

Creating a Map

Students will create a map detailing the routes of high-speed trains worldwide. An exemplary map will meet the following criteria:

- Title tells the purpose/content of the map, is clearly distinguishable as the title (e.g., larger letters, underlined, etc.)
- All items are labeled and located correctly
- Legend is easy to find and contains a complete set of symbols, including a compass rose
- All features on map are drawn to scale and the scale used is clearly indicated on the map
- All words on the map are spelled and capitalized correctly
- Student always uses color appropriate for features (e.g., blue for water; black for labels, etc.) on map
- Map includes properly documented sources

High-Speed Trains

High-speed trains were originally developed in the 1960s and 1970s, as rail operators looked for ways to compete with cheap air travel. The trains operate much faster than normal rail traffic, usually at 125 miles per hour (200 kph) or higher. High-speed trains are designed primarily for passenger services, but some also carry freight. Countries around the world have used new technology to improve their rail systems, including monorails and maglev trains powered by magnetic fields.

ARCTIC OCEAN

NORTH AMERICA

ATLANTIC OCEAN

PACIFIC OCEAN

SOUTH AMERICA

BRADFORD, PENNSYLVANIA

The world's first monorail opened in 1872 to link the towns of Bradford and Derrick City in Pennsylvania. The cars had to be carefully balanced so they did not tip off the single rail. On one journey, when the train had to carry a piano, the crew borrowed a cow to counterbalance the weight.

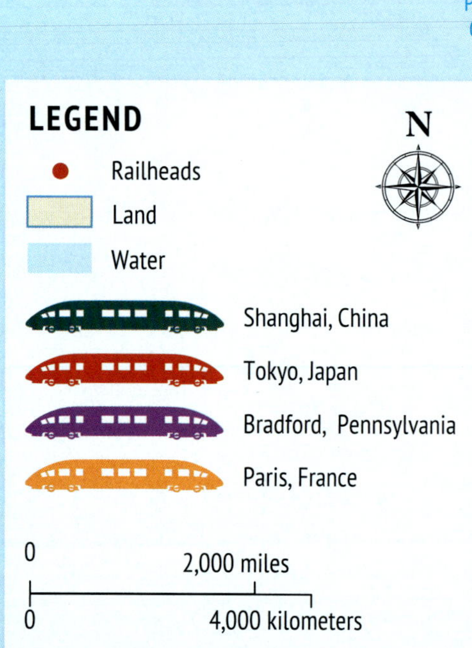

PARIS, FRANCE

One of the first high-speed trains was the French electric *Train à Grande Vitesse* (TGV). The first line opened in 1981, between Paris and Lyon. Paris is now the hub of a network connecting major French cities. By 2011, TGVs reached the highest speeds of any conventional rail networks in the world, regularly reaching speeds of up to 220 mph (350 kph).

TOKYO, JAPAN

The Japanese built the first "bullet train" in 1964. This electrically powered train connected Tokyo and Shin-Osaka. There are now many other lines, but the original line is the most used high-speed train route in the world, having carried more than 5.3 billion passengers since its opening. Modern Japanese high-speed trains, called *Shinkansen*, have maximum speeds of up to 200 mph (320 kph).

SHANGHAI, CHINA

In 2002, the first high-speed maglev railroad opened to connect Shanghai to its airport at Pudong. Maglev technology works by using repelling magnetic currents to lift the train slightly above the track and propel it forward. In 2015, an experimental Japanese maglev train reached a speed of 375 mph (603 kph).

ACTIVITIES

Google Maps

High-Speed Trains

Examine the map of railhead centers.

1. Analyze why the railheads might be centered where they are. Why would high-speed trains be preferable over conventional trains in such places? Support your theories.
2. Why do you think most of the countries that have developed high-speed trains are centered in Europe, North America, China, and Japan? What factors might prevent their introduction in South America, Africa, and Australia?

RUBRIC

Creating a Timeline

Students will explore the history of personal computers and create a timeline to present their research connected to this topic. An exemplary timeline will meet the following criteria:

- Includes the most significant events pertaining to the topic to be compared and analyzed
- Includes interesting events
- Uses accurate information for all events, including date, location, and major details
- Orders the events in a chronological sequence
- Describes each event with accurate, vivid, and specific details
- Presents the topic from three or more perspectives
- Inspires the reader to ask thoughtful questions regarding the events and perspectives presented in the timeline
- Uses correct spelling, grammar, and punctuation
- Presents the timeline in a visually attractive and striking manner
- Presents the timeline in a neat, organized manner that is logical and easy to follow
- Uses creativity to present the timeline in an engaging manner
- Effectively communicates historical information relating to the topic
- Supports each event with reliable sources
- Includes a correctly formatted bibliography of all sources used to create the timeline

Birth Of Personal Computers

Personal computers (PCs) are familiar in homes all over the world. People use PCs to play games, send emails, manage accounts, shop, buy theater, movie, and concert tickets, and engage with social media.

It is difficult to imagine a world without PCs, yet they are relatively new. The first fully electronic computer was built in 1946 at the University of Pennsylvania. Called the Electronic Numerical Integrator and Calculator (ENIAC), it contained 18,000 vacuum tubes. Such machines filled large rooms and were unreliable because of tube failures. The invention of the transistor in 1947 offered a smaller, dependable replacement for the vacuum tube. The invention of the integrated circuit in 1958 made miniaturization possible.

In 1975, a computer appeared that was affordable and small enough to use at home. The Altair 8800 cost just $395 in kit form. The device had no monitor, keyboard, or printer and just 256 bytes of memory. Users programmed it by means of switches on the front of the box. They read the output from flashing lights on a panel.

Computer Software

Computer programs run applications such as word processing or games. They work only if a computer is able to communicate with a storage device such as a disk drive or the Cloud. This process requires special software in the form of an operating system.

The Altair 8800 measured 17 x 18 x 7 inches (43 x 46 x 18 cm) and had a 2 MHz microprocessor.

In 1972, U.S. computer scientist Gary Kildall devised PL/M (Programming Language/Microprocessor) to allow engineers to write programs for the read-only memory (ROM) of the Intel 4004 processor. The following year, Kildall wrote software that allowed the user to read and write data files stored on a disk. This CP/M (Control Program/Microcomputer) was the first operating system for small computers. A rival system, Disk Operating System (DOS), was developed by U.S. computer programmer Bill Gates of Microsoft in 1980. As MS-DOS, this operating system came to dominate the market. WordStar, launched in 1979, was the first popular word-processing program.

Smaller And Cheaper

Computers remained expensive until 1980, when English engineer Clive Sinclair designed the ZX80. In the United States, the ZX80 cost $199.95 ready-made. It had 1 kilobyte of random-access memory (RAM), and had a soft plastic keyboard. It connected to a TV receiver. Sinclair followed the ZX80 a year later with the more powerful ZX81. It used audiocassette tapes for storage.

IBM introduced its first small computer in 1981, coining the term "personal computer." Within a year or two, rival manufacturers were marketing cheaper imitations, known as "IBM clones." All of them resembled the IBM PC and used MS-DOS. All modern PCs are the direct descendants of those "clones."

Growth of Microsoft

One of the most important companies in the development of the PC was Microsoft. The firm was founded in Albuquerque, New Mexico, in April 1975 by two childhood friends, Paul Allen and Bill Gates. Both had dropped out of university, but both were interested in computers. After reading an article in the magazine *Popular Mechanics*, they produced their first product. This was a version of the computer language BASIC for the Altair 8800. In 1979, the company moved to Washington State, where it was easier to recruit skilled workers. In 1980, IBM prepared to launch a personal computer. Microsoft provided the Microsoft Disk Operating System (MS-DOS), which Gates and Allen actually purchased from another computer manufacturer. As the IBM PC came to lead the market, MS-DOS became the world's main operating system.

ACTIVITIES

Document

Altair 8800 Article, 1975

Examine the article in *Popular Electronics* that inspired Bill Gates to start one of the most famous companies in the world.

1. Why do you think this article had such an effect on Bill Gates and Paul Allen? What did they design as a direct result of this article? Assess the importance of this product. Could they have predicted the effect they were to have on the emerging computer age?
2. The Altair 8800 is described as being the "most powerful minicomputer project ever presented." The computer was still only available in kit form. Do you think the price tag of "under $400" would have attracted many people to purchase it? Support your conclusions.

Weblink

Personal Computer History: 1975–1984

Appraise the weblink on the early history of personal computers.

1. The first personal computers were kits that people could build themselves. Assess the likelihood of this being possible in 2018. What type of technology were these early kits using?
2. What were the most significant events in the 1980s that led to the development of the computer? What types of function were these early computers able to perform?

Shuttles and Space Stations

Plans for the space shuttle, or Space Transportation System (STS), date back to 1972. NASA wanted a reusable cargo-carrying rocket. It was hoped the shuttle would fly about 50 missions a year, but the actual average was about eight.

At launch, a shuttle had three parts—the orbiter, an external tank, and solid rocket boosters. The airplanelike orbiter had three main engines fueled by liquid oxygen and liquid hydrogen. The flight deck had seats for up to seven crew, and a lower deck served as living quarters, gym, and bathroom. The 59-foot (18-m) payload bay carried up to 27.6 tons (25 metric tons). A robot arm called the Remote Manipulator System deployed and retrieved payloads and acted as a "ladder" for space walks.

Shuttle Launch

Two minutes after lift off, the boosters fell away into the sea, from where they were recovered for reuse. As soon as the orbiter was in Earth orbit, about six minutes later, the crew jettisoned the external tank, which burned up as it reentered the atmosphere. At the end of a mission, the crew retrofired the maneuvering rockets to slow down the craft. It reentered Earth's atmosphere at an altitude of about 75 miles (120 km). From a speed of about Mach 25, the orbiter slowed down, the thermal tiles on the wings and fuselage glowing red hot from the heat generated by friction with the air. The craft landed at a speed of about 200 miles per hour (320 kph).

NASA built six shuttles. The first, *Enterprise*, was used for tests in 1977, and never went into space. In 1981, *Columbia* became the first shuttle to make an orbital flight, followed by *Challenger* in 1983, *Discovery* in 1984, and *Atlantis* in 1985.

The shuttle's external tank held extra fuel and had 148-foot (45-m) solid rocket boosters attached to either side.

In 1986, on mission 25, *Challenger* exploded soon after launch, killing all seven crew members. A leak from a booster ignited the fuel in the external tank. NASA built a new shuttle, *Endeavour*, in 1992. In 2003, *Columbia* disintegrated just 16 minutes before it was due to land. The accident was caused by a piece of foam that had hit and damaged the shuttle's wing shortly after liftoff. All the crew died. After a refit, *Discovery* flew to the International Space Station (ISS) in July 2005. The shuttle was used to resupply the ISS until the shuttle program ended in 2011.

Space Stations

In the 1960s, the United States and the USSR competed over space exploration. In the 1970s, both powers began to treat space as a resource. This approach meant staying in space for much longer periods of time, which requires an orbiting laboratory, or space station. The USSR launched the first station, *Salyut 1*, in 1971. This was followed by six further Salyuts and finally, in 1986, the *Mir* space station. Meanwhile, NASA created the Skylab project. *Skylab* was visited by three missions during 1973 before burning up in Earth's atmosphere in 1979. In 1998, construction of the ISS began as a joint venture between NASA, the Russian Space Agency, and the European Space Agency (ESA), with smaller contributions from many other countries. It has been continuously occupied since 2000 by astronauts and scientists from at least 17 nations.

Space Stations

A space station in orbit is, in effect, continuously falling toward Earth, but is traveling forward so fast that Earth's surface curves away as the craft moves forward. Both the space station and its contents are falling at the same rate, so there appears to be no gravity, resulting in a condition called **weightlessness** or zero gravity. In fact, gravitation in orbit is only slightly less than that on Earth. Space stations have been used to produce perfect crystals and other materials undistorted by gravity, and to study the effects of weightlessness on organisms. Electricity for space stations and satellites is provided by **solar panels**, or arrays. These use heat from the Sun to create an electric current to charge the station's batteries. The solar panels of the ISS span 4,000 square feet (375 square meters). They turn to point toward the Sun so they receive maximum solar power.

ACTIVITIES

Video

Station Life

Watch the video of life on the International Space Station (ISS) and learn how research has helped scientists to understand more about life on Earth.

1. How does a better understanding of how a lack of gravity affects fluids, flames, and materials help scientists to make more efficient combustion engines, better portable medical diagnostics, lighter alloys, and buildings that are more resistant to earthquakes? Summarize the processes.
2. Why is it important for astronauts to take physical exercise while they are in space? What do you think happens to the internal organs of the body if they are exposed to long periods of weightlessness?

Weblink

The International Space Station

Read the weblink on the International Space Station (ISS).

1. Summarize the stated purpose of the ISS. Discuss whether the $100 billion it cost to build was justified.
2. Besides the Space Shuttle, what other spacecraft have visited the ISS? Could robotic technology eventually replace human astronauts on the ISS, If so, assess whether or not that would seem to negate the original purpose of human space travel. Justify reasons for or against.

RUBRIC

Writing a Comparative Essay

Students will analyze the structure and properties of the superconducting buckminsterfullerene, "buckyballs," and the structure and composition of Richard Buckminster Fuller's patented geodesic structures and then write a comparative essay based on their analysis and conclusions. An exemplary comparative essay will meet the following criteria:

- Consists of a one-paragraph introduction, two or more body paragraphs, and a one-paragraph conclusion
- Introduction includes an engaging lead statement about the topic of the essay, more detailed information about the chosen topic, and a one-sentence thesis that specifically states the essay's argument
- Each body paragraph includes a topic sentence that refers to and supports the thesis, textual evidence of the argument, and an analysis of this evidence
- Body paragraphs end with a transition to the next paragraph
- Conclusion refers to the topic of the essay and the points presented in the body paragraphs, and restates the thesis
- Provides a thorough analysis of the topics in question
- Presents a clear, specific thesis that indicates a high level of critical engagement
- Organizes ideas in a logical manner
- Communicates arguments in a clear, effective manner
- Uses correct spelling, punctuation, and grammar
- Properly integrates any quotations used
- Correctly cites all sources used
- Correctly formats bibliography

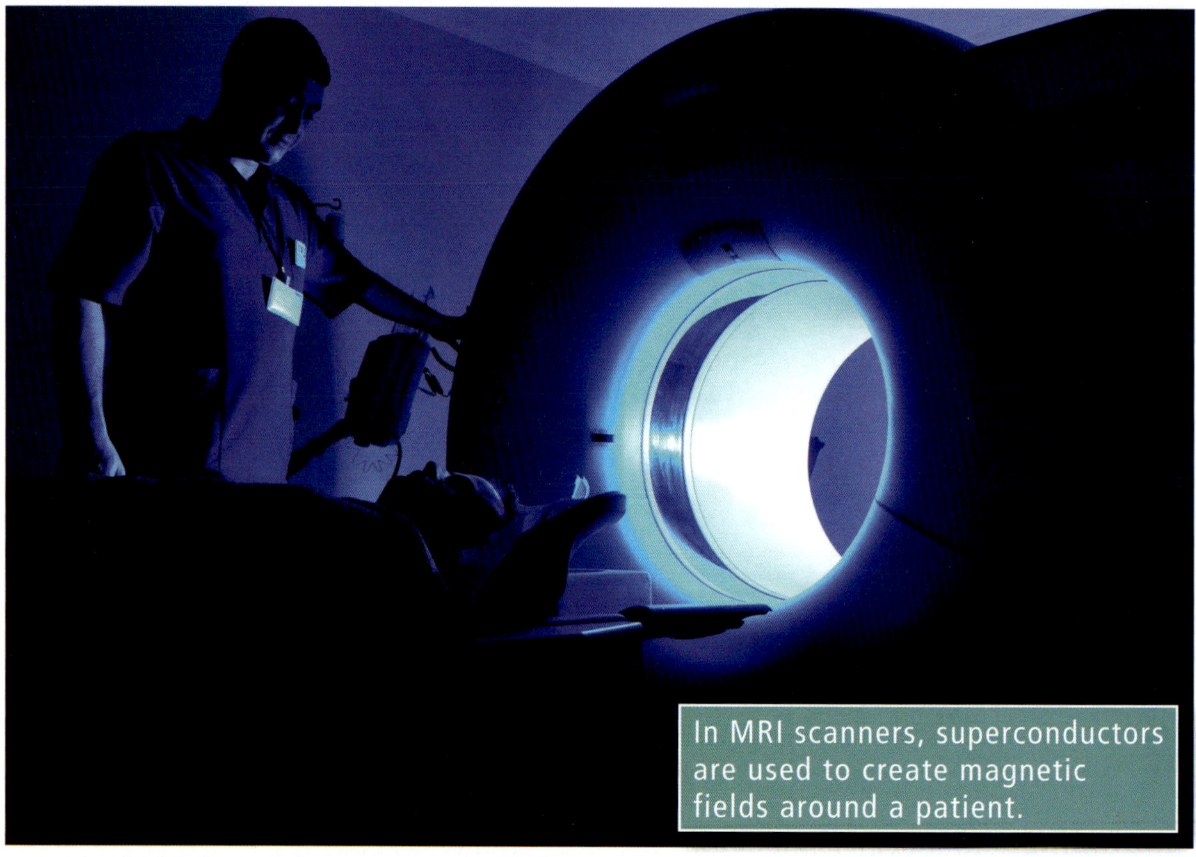

In MRI scanners, superconductors are used to create magnetic fields around a patient.

Superconductors

A superconductor is a substance that offers no resistance to the flow of electricity. The existence of superconductors was discovered by chance in 1911, when Dutch physicist Heike Kamerlingh Onnes cooled mercury to the temperature of liquid helium. Its resistance disappeared. For many years, scientists believed that superconductivity occurred only at temperatures close to absolute zero (0 Kelvin), which is equivalent to -459.67° Fahrenheit (-273.15° Centigrade). The temperature below which superconductivity occurs is known as the transition temperature (Tc). Most type-I superconductors, the first to be identified, are metals or metalloids, which have properties intermediate between those of metals and nonmetals. They superconduct only at very low temperatures. Some alloys and metal compounds classed as type-II superconductors have a higher Tc, especially when subjected to extremely high pressure. Until 1985, the highest Tc known at normal pressure was 23.2 K (-481.91°F, -249.95°C), for an alloy of niobium.

A Burst of Research

A breakthrough came in 1986, with the discovery of "high-temperature" superconductivity. Physicists Alex Müller and German Georg Bednorz worked at IBM Zürich. In 1983, they began experimenting with **ceramics**.

Ceramics seemed unlikely candidates for superconductivity, because they are often used as insulators. However, Müller and Bednorz found a barium–lanthanum–copper oxide with a Tc of about 35 K (-460.67°F, -238.15°C). The discovery raised the possibility of much higher transition temperatures, and it stimulated more research.

Within months, several laboratories had managed to raise the Tc to 39 K (-453.47°F, -234.15°C) by substituting strontium for barium. The Tc continued to rise during the 1980s and 1990s, as physicists tried to find a high-temperature superconductor. Low-temperature superconductors had to remain immersed in liquid helium, which is inconvenient and expensive to use. The liquid nitrogen used to refrigerate high-temperature superconductors, in contrast, is cheaper, plentiful, and easy to use.

Liquid nitrogen is used to preserve samples in chemistry and biology laboratories.

20
HEXAGONS
The number of hexagonal sections in a buckyball. Together with 12 pentagons, they form a structure resembling a soccer ball

-454°F
(-270°C)
The temperature at which helium becomes liquid and can insulate superconductors

While many scientists continued investigating ceramics, others turned in a new direction. They discovered superconducting properties in “buckyballs,” the nickname of buckminsterfullerene, discovered in 1985. A buckyball is a form, or allotrope, of carbon. In 1991, workers at AT & T Bell Laboratories mixed buckyballs with potassium (K) to make a superconductor at about 18 K (-491.27°F, -255.15°C). In 1993, scientists made a ceramic compound with a Tc of 133 K (-284.27°F, -140.15°C). In 2015, hydrogen sulfide was discovered to have a Tc of 203 K (-94°F, -70°C). However, this was only under very high pressure, which makes it impractical for use. Scientists around the world continue with the elusive quest to raise the Tc of superconductors.

ACTIVITIES

Document

Geodesic Dome

Study the Richard Buckminster Fuller’s Patented Geodesic Structures

1. Examine Fuller’s diagrams for geodesic domes and compare them to diagrams of buckminsterfullerene (C60). Are the “design scientist’s” drawings similar to the molecular structure of buckminsterfullerene? Describe their similarities and differences.
2. In the 1960s, several leading nuclear physicists were convinced that Fuller’s design for his geodesic domes explained the fundamental structure of the atomic nucleus, and was the basis of all matter. Assess the evidence and argue the case for and against.

Weblink

Why the Discovery of Room-Temperature Superconductors Would Unleash Amazing Technologies

Analyze this weblink on room-temperature superconductors.

1. Summarize the benefits of room-temperature superconductors. What could the main advantages be? Why have superconductor applications so far been limited to usage where the components of a system can be cooled to absolute zero?
2. How close have scientists come to achieving room-temperature superconductivity? Assess the drawbacks of these so-called high-temperature superconductors?
3. Describe the ongoing research for the elusive room-temperature superconductor.

The HST revealed vast pillars of gas and dust where new stars are forming.

The Hubble Space Telescope

Since Galileo first pointed his telescope at the Moon in 1610, what astronomers can see in space has been obscured by Earth's atmosphere. For this reason, they built observatories on mountaintops, where the air is thinner and cleaner. Then, in 1990, NASA launched a telescope into space, where there is no air to obscure the view.

The Hubble Space Telescope (HST) is named for U.S. astronomer Edwin Hubble, who dominated the science for more than 50 years in the first half of the twentieth century. Begun in 1977, the HST was completed in 1985, and placed in orbit by the space shuttle *Discovery* in early 1990. It follows an almost circular orbit 377 miles (607 km) above Earth, and was designed to be upgradeable, with instruments being renewed and others added. Space shuttle missions fixed early problems with the telescope and its instrumentation.

A Telescope in Space

The HST is an aluminum cylinder 43 feet (13 m) long and 14 feet (4.3 m) across. Electric power comes from two 40-foot (12-m) solar panels. Two high-gain antennas transmit signals to ground control at the Goddard Space Flight Center in Maryland. The cylinder houses a reflecting telescope with a prime mirror 94.5 inches (2.4 m) across. Clever optics "fold" the light path back on itself so that, although the telescope is only 21 feet (6.4 m) long, it is equivalent to a telescope with an overall length of 189 feet (57.6 m). In addition to the visual telescope, HST also carries five detectors of various types.

Correcting the View

The first images from the HST were disappointing because the prime mirror was faulty due to errors in testing during manufacture. In December 1993, the crew on the space shuttle *Endeavour* fitted the HST with a device called a Corrective Optics Space Telescope Axial Replacement (COSTAR). Together with a new wide-field camera, it fixed the problem. At once, the HST began to produce some startling images. Its faint-object camera could record objects 50 times fainter than anything that had ever been visible to astronomers from the ground.

Looking Into the Past

In July 1994, fragments of the comet Shoemaker-Levy 9 crashed into Jupiter, and the HST returned spectacular photographs of the momentous event. The telescope's spectrographs gathered important new data about the composition of Jupiter's atmosphere. By the end of 1995, the HST had taken a remarkable photograph called the Hubble Deep Field. Using exposures of 10 days, the Hubble Deep Field captured the light of faint galaxies in a small region of the constellation Ursa Major. These galaxies are 12 billion light-years away. Earth is only about 4.5 billion years old, so this means that the image shows objects as they were 7.5 billion years before Earth was formed.

The Hubble Deep Field was assembled from 342 separate images.

ACTIVITIES

Video

Hubble Memorable Moments: Comet Impact, 1994

Watch this video capturing one of Hubble's most memorable moments.

1. Why were astronomers keen to observe two extraterrestrial solar system bodies colliding? Describe what had happened to Comet Shoemaker-Levy 9 before it went on its collision course with Jupiter.
2. Summarize the preparations that were made before the expected collision to ensure that the HST was ready to capture the historic comet impact.
3. Evaluate the importance of the data revealed by the photos of the comet impact. Assess whether such information might protect Earth from the danger of comet impact in the future.

Weblink

About the Hubble Space Telescope

Examine this weblink and research further online.

1. Why did the launch of the HST mark the most significant advance in astronomy since Galileo's telescope? Explain the reasons.
2. NASA scientists have selected 13 representative topics from the thousands of Hubble images taken. Why do you think these particular topics were chosen? Assess the importance of the discoveries made in these areas.
3. The James Webb Space Telescope is due to come into operation soon. Compare the capabilities of both telescopes. Assess how they might complement each other in years to come.

RUBRIC

Researching for a Writing Assignment

Students will complete a thorough research process to prepare for a writing assignment on cloning, and organize their research in a logical manner that supports their writing. An exemplary research process will meet the following criteria:

- Creates a goal for the research, based on the topic and working thesis
- Creates specific, thoughtful, and inventive research questions that are relevant to the topic of the writing assignment
- Produces a list of categories, key words, and related ideas to effectively assist in researching
- Uses high-quality sources that pertain to the topic and come in a variety of formats, such as books, journals, primary sources, websites, and databases
- Uses sources that provide balanced research and various perspectives of the topic in question
- Takes notes to highlight the key facts and ideas in order to answer all research questions
- Extracts relevant, detailed information from the sources
- Writes notes in the student's own words
- Organizes the research notes in a clear and concise manner
- Analyzes the information and produces ideas and points to support the working thesis
- Uses an effective and suitable format to present all research
- Properly cites all sources used
- Uses quotations properly and ethically

Cloning

In 1892, German embryologist Hans Driesch watched the fertilized egg of a sea urchin divide into two identical cells under a microscope. Driesch then shook the cells in a beaker of seawater until they came apart. Each cell went on to develop into a sea urchin larva. Driesch had created identical twins, or clones.

In 1902, another German, Hans Spemann, split a two-cell salamander embryo. The two cells continued to divide, and developed and matured into identical adult animals. Over the next 40 years, Spemann investigated the possibilities of cloning. He predicted that it would be possible to create clones by transferring a **nucleus** from a differentiated adult cell into an egg cell from which the original nucleus had been removed. Instead of being a genetic blend of two parents, the embryo would be an exact replica of the animal from which the nucleus was taken.

Spemann's prediction became reality in two stages. In 1952, U.S. embryologists Robert Briggs and Thomas J. King took a cell from a frog embryo and transferred it into an unfertilized frog egg cell from which the nucleus had been removed. The clone developed normally.

The nucleus of a cell contains hereditary information that controls the cell's growth and reproduction.

Cloning a Mammal

The process to clone the first mammal, a sheep named Dolly, was complex. First, cells were taken from the udder of a Dorset ewe (1a). They were cultured and starved of nutrients before DNA replication began (2a). An egg was removed from a Scottish blackface ewe (1b), and its nucleus removed (2b). A nucleus was taken from one of the cultured Dorset ewe udder cells, and fused with the egg using electric shocks (3). The cell began to divide to form an embryo (4), which was transplanted into a receptive sheep (5). When Dolly was born (6), she was identical to the nucleus donor (1a).

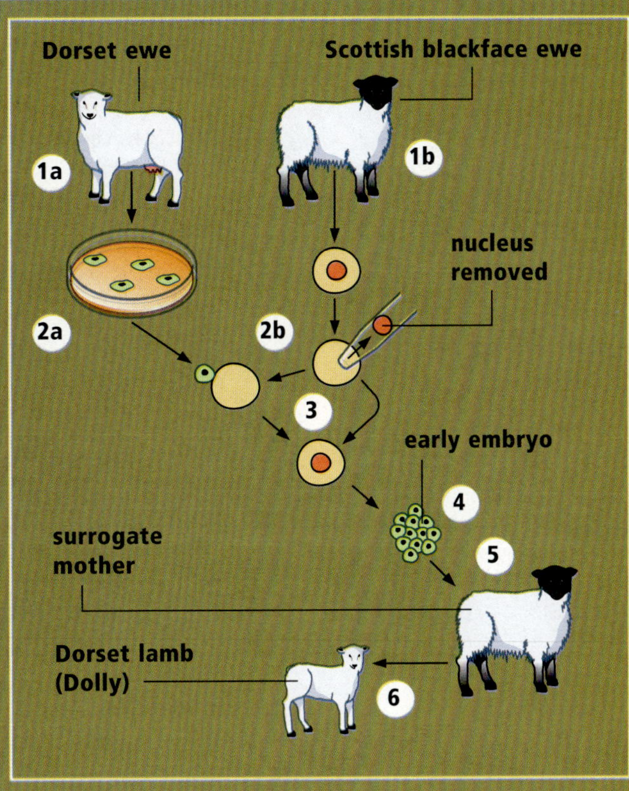

In 1958, scientists at Oxford University, England, led by John Gurdon, performed a similar procedure. This time, they used a nucleus from an adult cell. The fact that the donor cells were fully mature and differentiated was important. It proved that adult cells keep a full set of genetic material, despite the fact that only part of it is expressed. The nucleus of a cell from the intestine of a frog still "knew" how to make all the other types of cell that go to make up a whole frog. A few years later, in 1963, the term *clone* was coined by the Scottish geneticist John Burdon Sanderson Haldane. The word comes from the Greek for "twig."

Mammalian Clones

In 1977, a German scientist working at the University of Geneva caused a sensation when he claimed to have cloned three mice. Karl Illmensee claimed to have used similar nuclear transfer techniques to those previously used to create the amphibian clones. Other scientists were incredulous, because mammalian cells are much smaller than amphibian cells. Nobody could understand how he had managed to manipulate them. Illmensee was never able to satisfy his critics, and his claim came to be regarded as a fraud. The first reliably documented mammal clone, a sheep named Dolly, was produced in 1984.

ACTIVITIES

Transparency

Cloning a Mammal

Examine the diagram on cloning Dolly the Sheep.

1. Summarize the process by which Dolly was cloned. Why might it be beneficial to clone mammals?
2. What are the potential applications of cloned animals? What are the potential drawbacks? Assess the possible implications for human cloning.

Weblink

Cloning

Examine this weblink.

1. List the three different types of artificial cloning. Summarize what is achieved by the three different types. What might be the benefits of these types of cloning?
2. Describe the ethical issues related to cloning. Could humans ever be cloned? Argue the cases for and against.

Fossil fuels such as coal and natural gas produce carbon dioxide when they are burned.

The Greenhouse Effect

The natural greenhouse effect keeps Earth's average temperature about 30 degrees higher than it would otherwise be. The principles of the phenomenon were first described by French mathematician Jean Fourier, in 1827. In 1859, Irish physicist John Tyndall demonstrated that gases, including water vapor and carbon dioxide (CO_2), could trap heat.

Early Warning Signs

During the early twentieth century, scientists were aware that Earth's climate was enjoying a period of relative warmth, an interglacial period. Aware of the greenhouse role of CO_2, Swedish physical chemist Svante Arrhenius suspected that cooler **ice ages** might have been caused by reduced levels of atmospheric CO_2. He calculated the amount of CO_2 being released into the atmosphere by human activities. In 1896, Arrhenius first suggested that the world may experience global warming as a result of industrial emissions.

The idea was revived in 1939, by English hobby meteorologist Guy Stewart Callendar. He suggested that increases in temperatures and CO_2 levels were linked. The suggestion was rejected by many climatologists, who thought natural checks and balances would make such changes impossible. They insisted that any excess CO_2 would be absorbed by the oceans.

Rising sea levels caused by global warming lead to coastal flooding.

Scientists needed better models and more data, which became available over the latter part of the century. It became clear that levels of CO_2 in the atmosphere were rising rapidly. Scientists also uncovered layers of complexity relating to how Earth's climate systems work, making it almost impossible to give firm predictions. This uncertainty provided a loophole for those people who denied that there was a problem.

In the 1980s, scientific records around the world showed an increase in Earth's temperature, but the greenhouse effect was only one of many proposed causes. Climate models began to take account of variables such as ocean absorption and clouds. The year 1988 was a turning point. Globally, it was the hottest year on record. It was also the year that the public became aware of the possibility of global warming. By the early 1990s, human activity was producing 6.6 billion tons (6 billion metric tons) of CO_2 gas a year, mainly by burning fossil fuels. By 2000, most scientists had reached a general agreement that Earth is undergoing significant change, and that humans are contributing to the greenhouse global warming effect.

There were alarming predictions that this might mean rising sea levels, violent storms, floods, and droughts. Many governments took steps to limit their national output of greenhouse gases. In 1997, at Kyoto, Japan, and in 2015, in Paris, France, some nations made firm commitments to curb emissions. In 2017, the United States announced its decision to opt out of the Paris agreement, claiming that its terms damaged U.S. industry.

175
SIGNATORIES
The number of bodies that signed the Paris Agreement of 2015, including 174 countries and the European Union

---

17
WARMEST YEARS
The number of the 18 warmest years on record that have occurred since 2001

ACTIVITIES

Document

The Paris Agreement, 2015

Analyze the content of the Paris Agreement document.

1. What is the EU's overall assessment of the Paris Agreement? How might the signatories ensure that the objectives for C02 emission reductions are achieved? Describe the aim of the "ambition cycle."
2. Are countries' emissions reductions targets legally binding? What happens if one of the signatory countries fails to meet its agreed targets?

Weblink

What Is the Greenhouse Effect?

Analyze the weblink.

1. What effects have the burning of fossil fuels and deforestation had on the levels of greenhouse gases in Earth's atmosphere? Assess the argument that the greenhouse effect automatically leads to global warming?
2. Can climate change be reversed? What steps are being taken by the world's governments to reduce the amounts of harmful greenhouse gases released into the atmosphere?

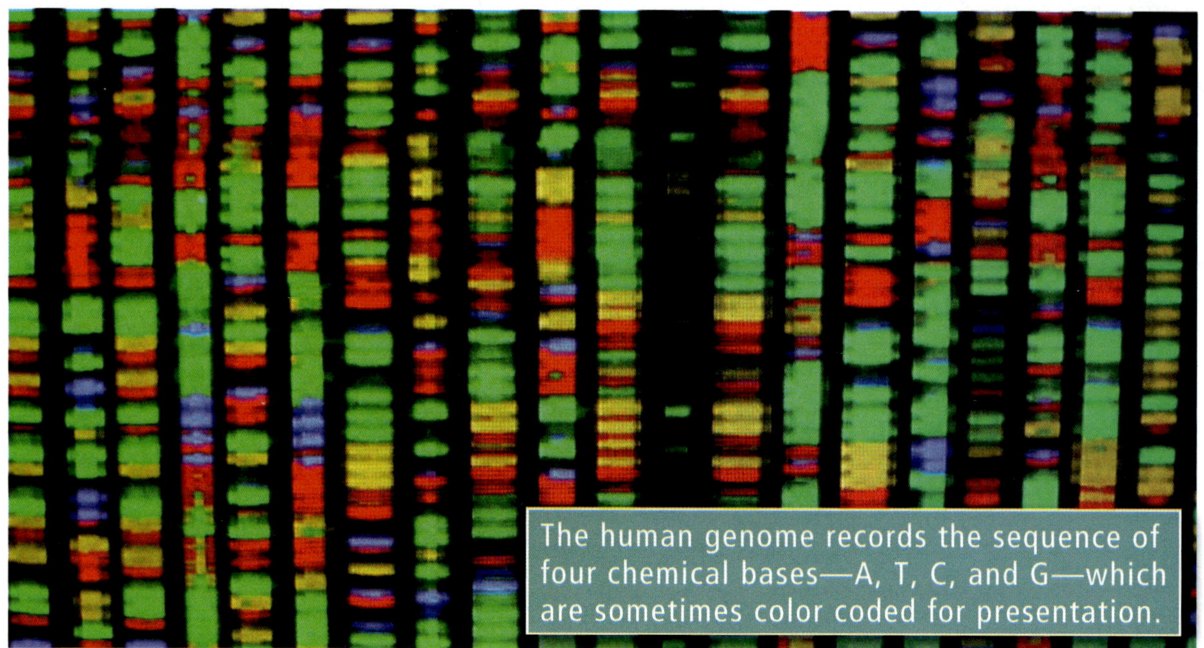
The human genome records the sequence of four chemical bases—A, T, C, and G—which are sometimes color coded for presentation.

The Human Genome Project

A genome is a complete set of genes, or genetic instructions, for making up an organism. All organisms inherit their genes from the previous generation, so the genome provides important information about ancestry. Faults or **mutations** in the genetic code often lead to medical conditions or disorders.

In 1913, the science of mapping genes began with the U.S. geneticist Alfred Sturtevant. Sturtevant figured out that the closer two genes were on a chromosome, the more likely it was that they would be passed on together when an organism bred. He used this principle, called genetic linkage, to map genes on the chromosomes of fruit flies.

Chromosomes are made from deoxyribonucleic acid (DNA), the structure of which was deciphered in 1953 by biophysicists James Watson and Francis Crick. The human genome is a code spelled out in the letters A, T, C, and G. The letters represent the chemical bases adenine, thymine, cytosine, and guanine, which link up to form the "rungs" of DNA's twisting, ladderlike structure.

Laying the Foundations

South-African born microbiologist Sydney Brenner spent his career studying the tiny roundworm *Caenorhabditis elegans*. He was able to follow the process of cellular division and to induce genetic mutations. Brenner's assistant, English scientist John Sulston, began mapping every cell in the roundworm's body, and tracing its development back to the embryo. By the late 1980s, the technology existed to start piecing together the sequences of DNA that collectively make up the genome of all biological organisms.

The Human Genome

Sulston's work sequencing the worm's genome put him at the forefront of research when the Human Genome Project was launched in 1990. The project was a collaboration between research institutes in several countries, led by the United States and Britain.

Its aims were to sequence the 3 billion or so letters of the human genetic code to identify all the genes contained within the sequence, and make them available for biological study. The project was predicted to take 15 years to complete. In fact, it took just 13 years.

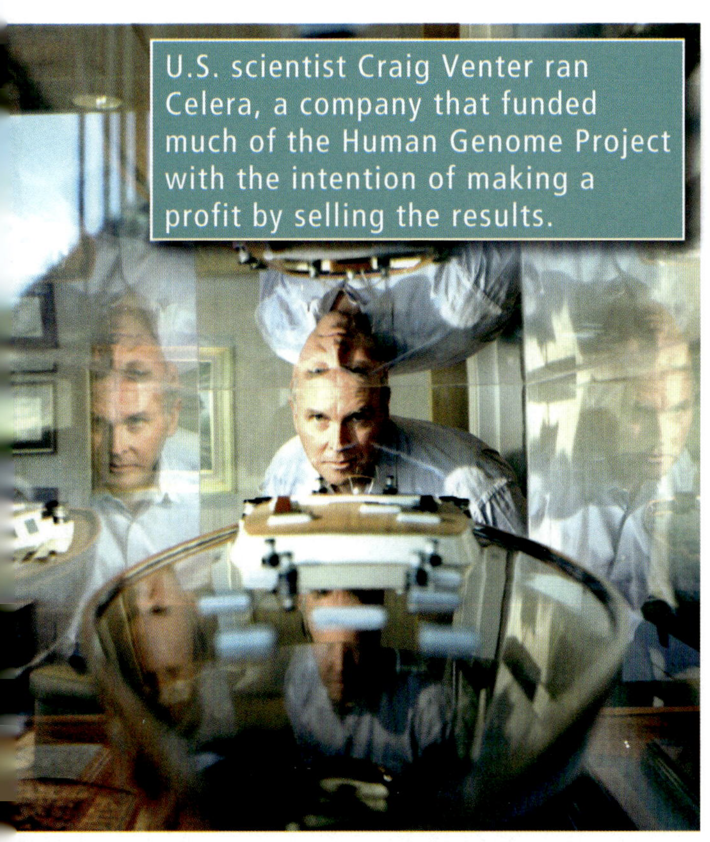

U.S. scientist Craig Venter ran Celera, a company that funded much of the Human Genome Project with the intention of making a profit by selling the results.

In England, Sulston's team decoded roughly one-third of the sequence, but most of the work was done in the United States. The speed with which the project was completed was thanks largely to advances in sequencing techniques pioneered by entrepreneur and scientist J. Craig Venter at the Institute for Genomic Research. While the science of the Human Genome Project advanced smoothly, the politics were troubled. During the project, an ethical rift opened between the privately funded branch of the project, represented by Venter, and the publicly funded branch, run principally by Sulston. Sulston objected to the idea that the human genome could be "owned" or patented, and a bitter row developed between the two scientists. In February 2001, two sets of results were published separately in the British journal *Nature* and the American *Science*. Both publications printed details of a first draft of the entire genome, a list of about 3 billion bases about 90 percent complete. The full sequence was published in 2003.

A Final Surprise

It may seem to most people that the human genome is incomprehensibly long. However, the scientists involved in sequencing it were surprised by how few genes it actually contains. The total of about 25,000 is far less than all previous estimates, which ranged from 50,000 to 120,000. In fact, it is only twice as many as the genome of a fruit fly.

ACTIVITIES

First Hand

The Human Genome: A Private vs. Public Battle

Review the weblinks on the human genome controversy.

1. Why did this important science project descended into public controversy?
2. Appraise the opposing views of Venter and Sulston. Which argument seems most convincing?
3. Assess whether such public controversy was good or bad for the reputation of the project. Is any publicity always good publicity?

Weblink

The Human Genome Project

Review the weblink on the Human Genome Project.

1. What is DNA? Give a brief description.
2. When and why was the Human Genome Project started? Summarize its aims.
3. Why might information about a person's DNA be useful? Describe how such knowledge could help to prevent crime or disease.

The internet is a network of linked servers around the world.

The World Wide Web

The World Wide Web uses telephone lines or radio to link computers in a network that extends across the world. It allows computer users instant access to billions of pages of documents as well as video, movies, and music. English computer scientist Tim Berners-Lee devised the Web in 1990.

Computer links had first been developed in the 1970s, for the Advanced Research Projects Agency (ARPA) of the U.S. Department of Defense, as a network known as ARPANET. ARPA began allowing outsiders to use its network in 1972. Stanford University launched a commercial version of ARPANET in 1974. In 1981, the City University of New York launched BITNET, which could be used by university scientists in the eastern United States who used IBM computers. EUNET followed in 1982. It linked computer networks in the United Kingdom, Scandinavia, and the Netherlands. A European version of BITNET was launched in 1984.

Birth of the Internet

As early as 1974, computer scientists at ARPA and Stanford University had devised a system called a transmission control **protocol**/internet protocol (TCP/IP). This allowed computers to send data between networks that used different formats of files. ARPA adopted TCP/IP in 1982. Now that networks were linked, email became possible. A computer that linked to a network is called a host, and email proved so popular that by 1984 there were more than 1,000 hosts.

In 1984, domain name servers were introduced. These computers store lists of domain names. Domain names include www (World Wide Web), ac (academic), edu (education), com (commercial), and gov (government), as well as national identifiers, such as uk (United Kingdom), de (Germany), and fr (France).

In 1985, the U.S. National Science Foundation established NSFNET to extend internet use to every U.S. campus. In 1988, NSFNET upgraded the network capacity from 56,000 to 1.544 million bytes per second. The number of internet users grew from about 5,000 in 1986 to 28,000 in 1987. In 1991, NSFNET allowed access to private computers. In 1992, Senator Al Gore introduced the High-Performance Computing Act, nicknamed the "information superhighway project" to encourage internet use in the United States.

Data is stored on huge servers that can be accessed from anywhere in the world.

The World Wide Web

In 1980, Tim Berners-Lee, a software developer at the European Organization for Nuclear Research (CERN), wrote a program that allowed computers to swap data using hypertext transfer protocol. Users could move easily between computer systems. After CERN approved further development in 1989, Berners-Lee wrote a program he named the World Wide Web. In August 1991, the program was published on the Internet for anyone to use. The Web grew slowly. By the end of 1993, it had only about 150 sites. In 1993, however, U.S. scientist Mark Andreessen released the first browser, Mosaic X, later renamed Netscape. Instead of typing in the address of a document, a user simply clicked on a hypertext link. Where the internet linked computers, the World Wide Web linked documents. As a result, the Web expanded far more quickly. By 2018, it had more than 1.3 billion websites.

ACTIVITIES

First Hand

Answers for Young People

Analyze Tim Berners-Lee's answers to questions from young people on all aspects of the World Wide Web .

1. Appraise Tim Berner-Lee's hopes for the future of the Web. Are these realistic aims? Is he right in saying "what is made of the Web is up to us?"
2. Why did Berners-Lee think there was a need for an information system that could be read from anywhere in the world on all types of computer?

Weblink

WWW—World Wide Web

Review the weblink on the World Wide Web.

1. Explain the difference between the Web and the Internet.
2. What are the three core technologies upon which the WWW is based? Summarize descriptions of each.
3. Explain how websites are accessed using their domain names and extensions. Give examples.

RUBRIC

Analyzing a Scientific Video

Students will watch and assess a video related to water, solar, or wind power, and write an analysis of the video. An exemplary video analysis will meet the following criteria:

- Identifies the purpose of the video
- Identifies the intended audience of the video
- Identifies the video as a primary or secondary source
- Discusses the scientific and social context of the video
- Describes how the content of the video is presented
- Summarizes the information and opinions presented in the video
- Analyzes the quality of the content presented in the video
- Assesses the effectiveness of the video
- Determines whether the images and graphics used in the video relate to the content
- Determines whether the video is easy to follow and understand
- Gives the analysis a clear and consistent purpose
- Organizes the analysis in a logical, effective manner
- Presents a strong, clear argument about the video
- Provides strong and accurate details to support the argument about the video
- Considers other perspectives on the purpose and effectiveness of the video
- Cites all sources used in the analysis

Future Energy

Wind has been used as a form of power since Roman times, and windmills were in widespread use on U.S. farms by the 1890s. The late twentieth century saw the development of efficient wind turbines. These turbines turn generators to produce electricity. French engineer G. Darrieus designed a turbine turning on a vertical axis in 1931. A prototype of the modern turbine, using blades similar to an aircraft propeller, was tested in Rutland, Vermont, in the 1940s, but broke. Following the oil crisis in the early 1970s, there was renewed interest in wind energy. The first successful propeller turbine was built near Sandusky, Ohio, in 1976.

Power of Water

The design of better turbines prompted renewed interest in water power. In the mid-nineteenth century, U.S. hydraulic engineer James B. Francis developed a device with blades curved to extract maximum power from moving water. Another device, the Pelton wheel, was designed in 1889. It has small cups mounted around its circumference that catch water and turn the wheel.

Hydroelectric power plants are like waterwheels on a vast scale. They consist of turbines placed in the path of a dammed river or a sea dam on a tidal estuary. The first such plant was built at Appleton, Wisconsin, in 1882. The Hoover Dam on the Arizona–Nevada border contains 17 Francis turbines. It was completed in 1936.

In the 1980s, tax concessions encouraged the building of "wind farms" in states such as California.

Large areas of solar panels absorb heat from the Sun, but are only practical in regions with a suitable climate.

Although they are cleaner and more sustainable than fossil fuels, wind and water power have their own problems. Most U.S. states do not have enough wind to generate all the power they need. About 90 percent of U.S. wind-generating capacity is limited to 12 states. Hydroelectric dams can be environmentally destructive. Building the Three Gorges Dam on the Yangtze River in China, for example, which opened in 2003, disrupted populations of species such as the highly rare Yangtze River Dolphin.

Energy from the Sun

Most of the world's energy comes indirectly from the Sun. This includes wind and water power and all fossil fuels. The Sun's energy can be used directly as heat, or can be converted into electricity with solar cells.

In 1887, German physicist Heinrich Rudolf Hertz found that light could be used to generate electricity. This phenomenon, called the photoelectric effect, led to the development of the first solar cell by Charles Fritts, in about 1883. It was not until silicon solar cells were developed by Russell Ohl in 1941 that producing electric power from the Sun became viable.

Today's solar power plants include one in the Mojave Desert near Barstow, California. A so-called power tower 295 feet (90 m) high collects the Sun's rays from 1,900 movable mirrors placed all around it on the ground. By 2016, there were 1.3 million solar installations in the United States. They generated enough electricity to power more than 6.5 million homes.

Power for the Future

For all their promise, renewable forms of energy, such as wind and water, generate only a tiny proportion of the world's power needs. With the global population expected to rise from 7.6 billion in 2018 to more than 9.8 billion by the middle of the twenty-first century, there is a pressing need to find new ways of both generating power and saving energy. Never has the role of scientists, inventors, and inventions been more vital to the survival of humankind.

ACTIVITIES

Video

Solar Powerplant in the Mojave Desert

Analyze the operations of a giant solar plant in the Mojave Desert.

1. Summarize how this giant solar plant works. Describe some of the challenges that such a process produces and explain the possible solutions.
2. How does the shape of the mirrors focus sunlight to create such extremes of heat energy?
3. Are some criticisms that sacrificing ecosystems for the sake of producing relatively small amounts of electricity justified? Defend the arguments.

Weblink

Energy Systems

Explore this link on sustainable energy for the future.

1. What does the term "alternative energy" refer to? Explain the categories and describe the individual sources.
2. Why are renewable resources more easily produced than finite natural resources? Summarize the basic processes involved in both cases.
3. How is the energy created by water, wind, the Sun, or any other natural resource distributed to consumers in the form of electricity? Describe the process.

Timeline of Scientific Discoveries

The later twentieth and early twenty-first centuries saw many advances in science and technology being made around the world. These are some of the most important breakthroughs. They cover a wide range of fields of science.

	1960–1965	1966–1971	1972–1977	1978–1983	1984–1989
Technology	**1961** Soviet cosmonaut Yuri Gagarin becomes the first human in space. **1964** John Kemeny and Thomas Kurtz invent computer language BASIC.	**1969** NASA's *Apollo 10* orbits the Moon, and *Apollo 11* makes the first manned Moon landing. *Apollo 12* also lands on the Moon.	**1975** U.S. engineer Edward Roberts markets the first personal computer, the Altair 8800. **1976** The *Viking 1* and *Viking 2* space probes land on Mars.	**1981** French railway company SNCF introduces the TGV. **1981** NASA's space shuttle, *Columbia*, makes its first flight.	**1984** Apple markets the first Macintosh computer. **1986** The Soviet Union launches the first permanently crewed space station, Mir.
Biology and Medicine	**1962** *Silent Spring*, U.S. naturalist Rachel Carson raises public awareness of the effects of chemical pesticides on the environment.	**1967** South African surgeon Christiaan Barnard performs the first successful heart transplant operation. The patient lives for 18 days with his new heart.	**1973** U.S. biologists Stanley Cohen and Herbert Boyer invent a method of cloning genetically engineered molecules in foreign cells.	**1983** French virologist Luc Montagnier and U.S. physician Robert Gallo identify the human immunodeficiency virus (HIV) that causes the disease AIDS.	**1984** Danish reproductive physiologist Steen Willadsen clones the first mammal, a sheep, using the nucleus of an embryonic sheep cell.
Physical Sciences/Math	**1964** U.S. radio astronomers Arno Penzias and Robert Wilson detect cosmic background microwave radiation, which convinces most astronomers that the universe began in an explosion called the big bang.	**1969** English chemist Dorothy Hodgkin uses X-ray crystallography and computers to determine the molecular structure of insulin.	**1974** U.S. scientists Mario Molina and F. Sherwood Rowland issue warnings about the damaging effect chemicals are having on the ozone layer around Earth.	**1978** The U.S. government bans the use of some chemicals as propellants in aerosol cans because they damage Earth's ozone layer.	**1988** U.S. climatologist James Hansen predicts that increased levels of "greenhouse gases" in Earth's atmosphere will lead to harmful global warming.

ACTIVITIES

1990–1995	1996–2000	2001–2006	2007–2012	2013–2018
1990 Space shuttle *Discovery* places the HST in orbit around Earth. **1990** English computer scientist Tim Berners-Lee begins to devise what becomes the World Wide Web.	**1997** NASA's space probe *Galileo* orbits Jupiter's moons Europa and Callisto.	**2005** After a seven-year trip, the Cassini–Huygens space probe reaches Saturn.	**2007** Apple introduces a touchscreen cell phone named the iPhone. **2009** NASA launches the Kepler telescope to search the sky for planets with the potential to support life.	**2015** The space probe *New Horizons* makes the first flyby of the dwarf planet Pluto.
1990 The Human Genome Project begins, directed by U.S. biophysicist James Watson. **1994** Genetically modified tomatoes called Flavr Savr are marketed in the United States.	**1996** Scottish biologist Ian Wilmut clones a sheep named Dolly. Two years later, Dolly gives birth to a lamb in the normal way.	**2004** Medical researchers in South Korea clone human embryos in order to obtain stem cells for therapeutic purposes only.	**2008** NASA reports that the thickest Arctic ice is melting, according to satellite data, thanks to warmer average global temperatures.	**2017** U.S. President Donald Trump announces his intention to withdraw the United States from the Paris Agreement on climate change.
1995 U.S. geophysicists Xiaodong Song and Paul Richards detect the rotation of Earth's solid inner core through computer analysis of seismic waves.	**1999** Russian researchers create element 114 by bombarding plutonium-244 with calcium-48 nuclei, and U.S. scientists create element 118 by fusing lead-208 with krypton-86, but it decays to form element 116.	**2004** Physicists from Penn State University announce a helium-based "supersolid" that flows through another material without friction.	**2008** The Large Hadron Collider, near Geneva, is forced to close down just nine days after opening. It is the world's largest and highest-energy particle accelerator.	**2015** Scientists confirm the existence of gravitational waves, deflections in space-time first predicted by Albert Einstein in the early 1900s.

Transparency

Timeline of Science Discoveries

Analyze important scientific discoveries from 1960 to 2018.

1. Why might these discoveries be featured in the timeline? What makes these particular discoveries important?
2. How do you think the general public would have viewed these discoveries when they were first revealed? How might their opinions have differed from those of scientists? Why?
3. What effect did these discoveries have on the field of science?
4. How might these discoveries have shaped the world today? What sources can be used to illustrate these effects?

Quiz

1 What atoms are used in the hydrogen bomb?

2 When was the first solid three-terminal transistor made?

3 Who carried out the first successful heart transplant?

4 Who were the first two people to walk on the Moon?

5 What was the first commercial personal computer?

6 How far above Earth does the Hubble Space Telescope orbit?

7 How many of the 18 warmest years on record have occurred since the year 2001?

8 About how many letters are there in the human genetic code?

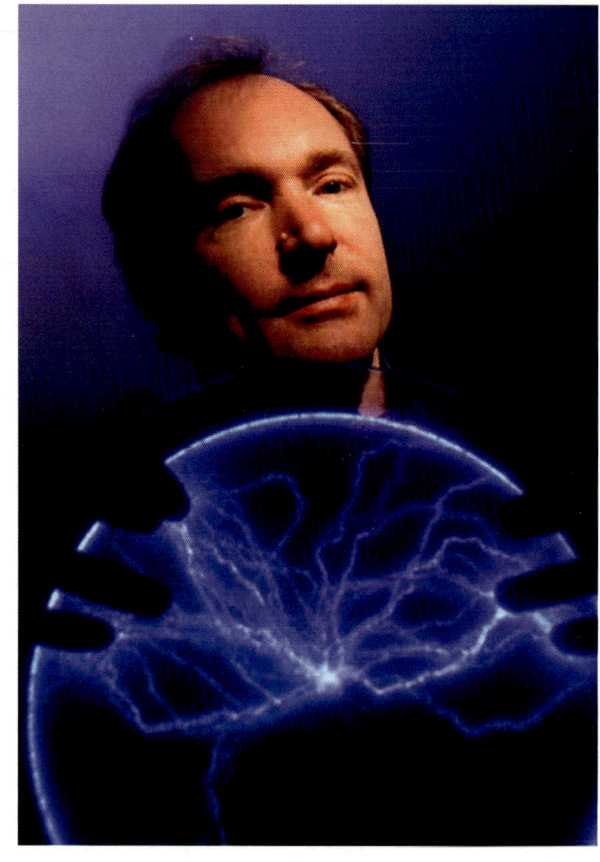

9 Which British scientist came up with the World Wide Web?

10 From where does most of Earth's energy indirectly come?

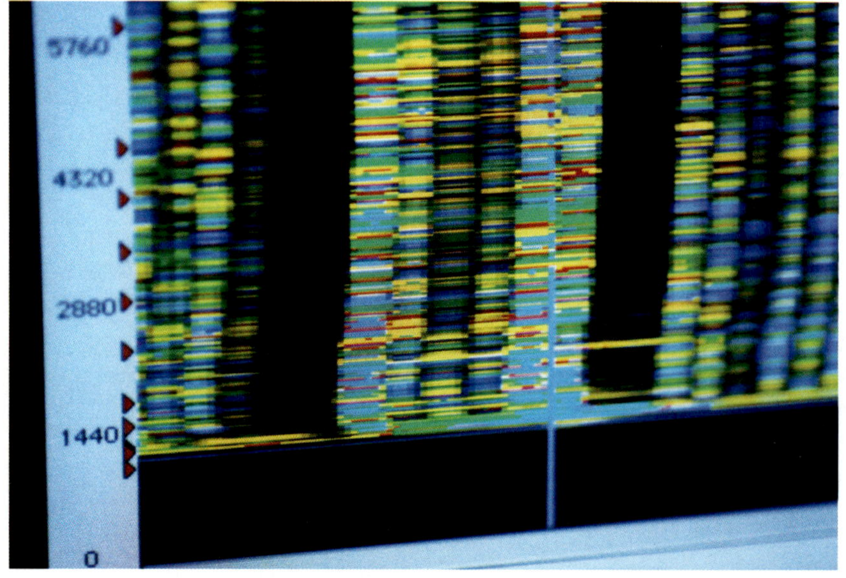

ANSWERS
1. Deuterium **2.** 1947
3. Christiaan Barnard
4. Neil Armstrong and Buzz Aldrin **5.** Altair 8800 **6.** 377 miles (607 km) **7.** 17
8. 3 billion
9. Tim Berners-Lee
10. The Sun

Study the Sources

The history of science is a complicated subject. Historians must be able to understand scientific processes as well as the ways in which history changes because of social, economic, political, or military pressures and opportunities. Adding to the difficulty, the people who recorded advances in the past often did not understand what was actually happening in the scientific developments they were describing.

Consider a major theme discussed in this book. Topics you could choose might be computers or space exploration. Use the internet to find at least two descriptions and at least two images of the topic. Note how people with different viewpoints portrayed different aspects as being important. Some people may be hostile to innovations, while others may be supportive, for example.

Compare the descriptions and images you find with this book. Technology is changing many aspects of life. Do you think historians in the twentieth and twenty-first centuries understood the true impact of the changes taking place? Why do you think it might have been difficult to appreciate developments?

Key Words

amplifier: an electronic device that increases the strength of an input current or voltage

ceramics: any of various hard, brittle, heat-resistant, and corrosion-resistant materials, particularly those based on clay

desertification: the gradual turning of farmland into desert by climate change

diodes: electronic components that allow current to flow in only one direction

ecosystem: a community of interacting living things and their physical environment

endoscope: a tubular medical instrument used to carry out visual examinations of hollow parts of the body

epilepsy: disorders that cause disturbances in electrical signaling in the brain

fusion: a process by which two or more atomic nuclei join together to make a heavier atom

galena: a blue-gray mineral of lead sulfide that forms cubic crystals and is a major source of lead

global warming: also called climate change, a general and long-term rise of the temperature of Earth's atmosphere

gyroscope: a device consisting of a spinning mass, typically a disk or wheel, mounted on a base so that its axis can turn freely, thus maintaining its orientation regardless of any movement of the base

Human Genome Project: an international scientific research mission to decipher the entire sequence of genes in the human genome

ice ages: periods of time when large areas of Earth's surface were covered with ice sheets

lasers: in medicine, devices that emit an intense beam of monochromatic radiation capable of producing immense heat and power when focused at close range

moon: a naturally occurring, relatively large body, in orbit around a planet

mutations: heritable changes in individuals' genetic material

NASA: a U.S. government agency set up in 1958 to design and implement the American space program

nucleus: a membrane-bound structure that contains hereditary information, and controls a cell's growth and reproduction

protocol: a standard way of communicating across a network

radar: acronym for "radio detection and ranging," a measuring instrument in which the echo of a pulse of microwave radiation is used to detect objects

solar panels: panels consisting of an array of solar or photovoltaic cells, which convert sunlight directly into electricity

transistor: a solid-state electronic device that amplifies a small signal current or voltage and turns it into a large output current

weightlessness: the absence of weight due to the lack of the force of gravity acting on a body

Index

LIGHTBOX

SUPPLEMENTARY RESOURCES

Click on the plus icon found in the bottom left corner of each spread to open additional teacher resources.

- Download and print the book's quizzes and activities
- Access curriculum correlations
- Explore additional web applications that enhance the Lightbox experience

LIGHTBOX DIGITAL TITLES

Packed full of integrated media

VIDEOS

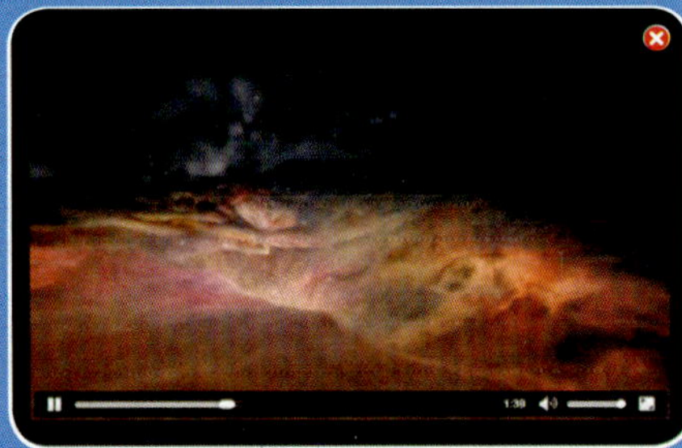

INTERACTIVE MAPS

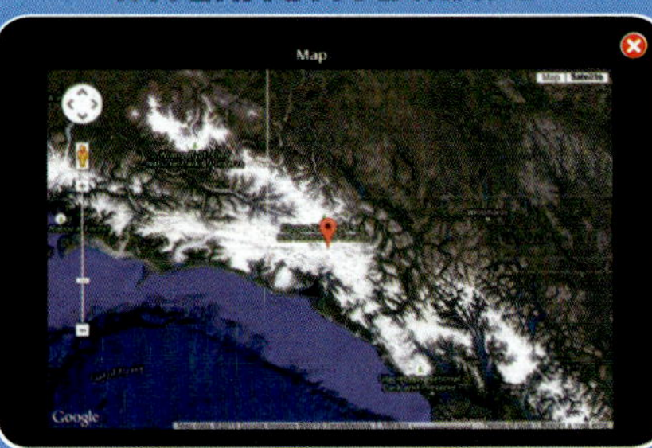

WEBLINKS

SLIDESHOWS

QUIZZES

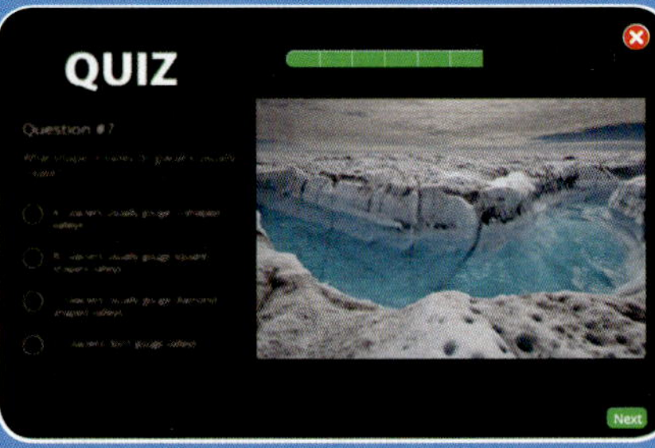

OPTIMIZED FOR

- ✓ TABLETS
- ✓ WHITEBOARDS
- ✓ COMPUTERS
- ✓ AND MUCH MORE!

Published by Smartbook Media Inc.
350 5th Avenue, 59th Floor New York, NY 10118
Website: www.openlightbox.com

First published by Brown Bear Books in 2009

Library of Congress Control Number: 2018941509

ISBN 978-1-5105-3769-9 (hardcover)
ISBN 978-1-5105-3770-5 (multi-user eBook)

Printed in Brainerd, Minnesota, United States
1 2 3 4 5 6 7 8 9 0 22 21 20 19 18

072018
121217

Project Coordinator: Heather Kissock
Art Director: Ana María Vidal

Every reasonable effort has been made to trace ownership and to obtain permission to reprint copyright material. The publisher would be pleased to have any errors or omissions brought to its attention so that they may be corrected in subsequent printings.

The publisher acknowledges Getty Images, Alamy, Shutterstock, iStock, and Newscom as its primary image suppliers for this title.